What's Wrong with This Picture?
Critical Thinking Exercises
in Geometry

Michael Serra

Key Curriculum Press
Innovators in Mathematics Education

Project Editor:	Christopher David
Editorial Assistant:	Lori Dixon
Editorial Consultant:	Curt Gebhard
Mathematical Content Reviewer:	Dudley Brooks
Production Editor:	Christine Osborne
Copyeditor:	Erin Milnes
Production Director:	Diana Jean Parks
Text Design and Composition:	Mike Hurtik
Illustrators:	Smolinski Studios, Ron Lipking
Art and Design Coordinator:	Caroline Ayres
Cover Designer:	Sherry Ahlstrom
Cover Illustration:	Ron Lipking
Prepress/Printer:	Data Reproductions
Executive Editor:	Casey FitzSimons
Publisher:	Steven Rasmussen

Key Curriculum Press
1150 65th Street
Emeryville, CA 94608
510-595-7000
editorial@keypress.com
http://www.keypress.com

Printed in the United States of America
10 9 8 7 6 5 4 3 2   08 07 06 05 04
ISBN 1-55953-584-9

Contents

Note to Teachers

You can trace the beginnings of this book to my classroom presentation and worksheet mistakes. All of us in the classroom have done it: Two-thirds of the way through a clever derivation, one of your students says, "Wait! Isn't that supposed to be 'minus x' instead of 'plus x'?" With a glimmer in your eye, you respond, "Ah, yes, very good, finally someone noticed. I was just checking to make sure you were paying attention."

Students love catching mistakes so much that I began creating exercises called "What's Wrong with This Picture?" In these exercises, I tell students up front that something is wrong. Students search for an error in the diagram or the mistake in the process of solving a problem, and they explain why it is a mistake. *Discovering Geometry* has a number of these exercises. They work as excellent drill and review of material and ask students to think differently in explaining their reasoning.

Each page in *What's Wrong with This Picture?* becomes a puzzle containing three or four pieces. Students are asked to look closely at each of the problems on the page because some are correct and some are not. If at least one is worked correctly and at least one is worked incorrectly, they must read more carefully, follow the reasoning, and explain why a particular problem is correctly worked and another is not. Sometimes all the problems seem to be incorrect and the search is to find the correct one. Sometimes all the problems seem to be correct, and the search is on for the error.

I believe that when students are given opportunities to be actively involved in their curriculum they become better problem solvers and develop a deeper understanding of the concepts. When concepts are discussed and debated in connection with a "story" that explains how and why these geometric properties came to be, students have a greater retention of the material.

I suggest a couple of possible approaches to using *What's Wrong with This Picture?* One possibility is to make a copy of a page and add it to the students' homework assignment. Students work on the problems at home, and when they return to class, spend five to ten minutes discussing their results with members of their group. Another approach is to use the exercises as an in-class warm-up. The print size is large enough so that you can make overhead transparencies of the pages. Display one of the pages on the overhead screen as students enter the classroom. While you take attendance, students can work on the problems individually, and then discuss the problems with their group members.

What's Wrong with This Picture

Complementary, Supplementary, and Vertical Angle Properties

At least one of the boxes below is correct, and at least one is incorrect. Identify which boxes are correct and which are incorrect. For each incorrect box, explain why it is incorrect.

1

A, B, and C are collinear.

72°

118°

B

C

A

2

IT TAKES ABOUT ELEVEN AND A HALF DAYS FOR A MILLION SECONDS TO ELAPSE.

3

$\overleftrightarrow{AB} \perp \overleftrightarrow{CD}$

True

B

C

48° E

42°

D

A

4

$\overleftrightarrow{AB}$ intersects $\overleftrightarrow{CD}$ at E.

D

37°

B

A

39° E

False

C

What's Wrong with This Picture

Complementary, Supplementary, and Vertical Angle Properties

At least one of the boxes below is correct, and at least one is incorrect. Identify which boxes are correct and which are incorrect. For each incorrect box, explain why it is incorrect.

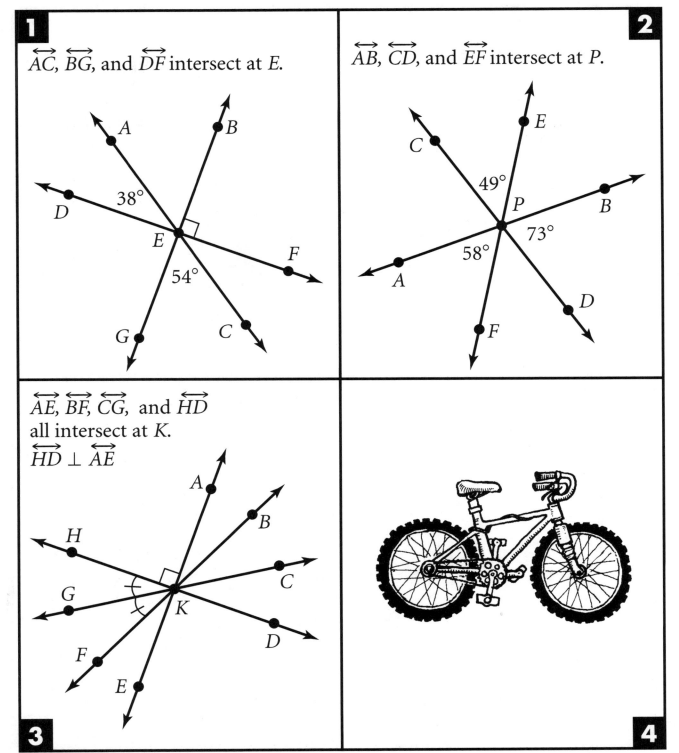

1

$\overleftrightarrow{AC}$, $\overleftrightarrow{BG}$, and $\overleftrightarrow{DF}$ intersect at E.

A   *B*

D   38°

E

F

54°

G   *C*

2

$\overleftrightarrow{AB}$, $\overleftrightarrow{CD}$, and $\overleftrightarrow{EF}$ intersect at P.

C   *E*

49°

P   *B*

73°

58°

A

F   *D*

3

$\overleftrightarrow{AE}$, $\overleftrightarrow{BF}$, $\overleftrightarrow{CG}$, and $\overleftrightarrow{HD}$ all intersect at K.
$\overleftrightarrow{HD} \perp \overleftrightarrow{AE}$

A

B

H

C

G

K

D

F

E

4

What's Wrong with This Picture

3

At least one of the boxes below is correct, and at least one is incorrect. Identify which boxes are correct and which are incorrect. For each incorrect box, explain why it is incorrect.

1 $\overleftrightarrow{PT}, \overleftrightarrow{QU}, \overleftrightarrow{RV},$ and $\overleftrightarrow{SW}$ are concurrent at X. $\overleftrightarrow{PT} \perp \overleftrightarrow{VR}$

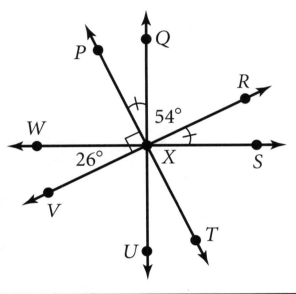

2 $P, Q,$ and R are collinear. $\overrightarrow{QS} \perp \overrightarrow{QT}$

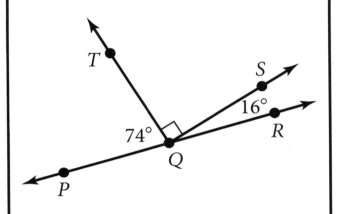

3 $A, F,$ and E are collinear. $\overrightarrow{FC}$ bisects $\angle BFD$.

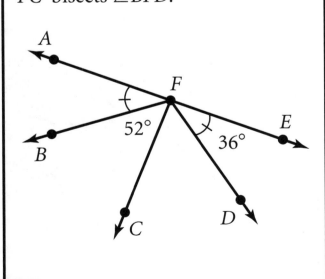

4

What's Wrong with This Picture

Complementary, Supplementary, and Vertical Angle Properties

At least one of the boxes below is correct, and at least one is incorrect. Identify which boxes are correct and which are incorrect. For each incorrect box, explain why it is incorrect.

1 $\overleftrightarrow{AD}$, $\overleftrightarrow{BE}$, and $\overleftrightarrow{CG}$ are concurrent at H.

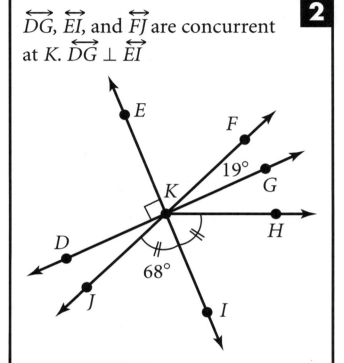

2 $\overleftrightarrow{DG}$, $\overleftrightarrow{EI}$, and $\overleftrightarrow{FJ}$ are concurrent at K. $\overleftrightarrow{DG} \perp \overleftrightarrow{EI}$

Problem

True or false?

$$1999^2 - 1998^2 = \frac{49^2 - 48^2}{49 + 48}$$

Solution

True

4 $\overleftrightarrow{RV}$, $\overleftrightarrow{SW}$, $\overleftrightarrow{TX}$, and $\overleftrightarrow{UY}$ are concurrent at Z.

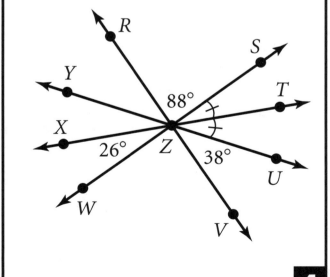

3

What's Wrong with This Picture

Angle Properties and Parallel Properties

At least one of the boxes below is correct, and at least one is incorrect. Identify which boxes are correct and which are incorrect. For each incorrect box, explain why it is incorrect.

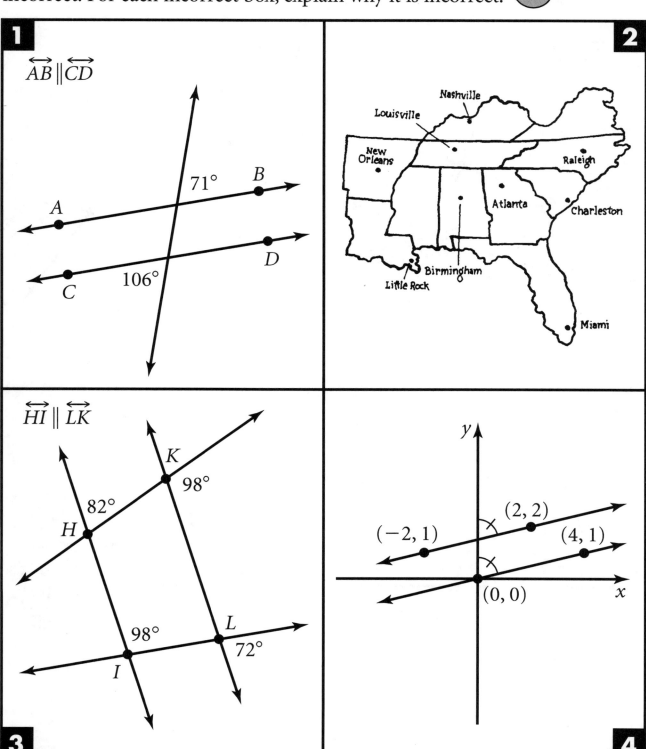

1

$\overleftrightarrow{AB} \parallel \overleftrightarrow{CD}$

71°

B

A

D

106°

C

2

Nashville

Louisville

New Orleans

Raleigh

Atlanta

Charleston

Birmingham

Little Rock

Miami

3

$\overleftrightarrow{HI} \parallel \overleftrightarrow{LK}$

K

98°

82°

H

98°

L

72°

I

4

y

(2, 2)

(−2, 1)

(4, 1)

(0, 0)

x

What's Wrong with This Picture

Angle Properties and Parallel Properties

At least one of the boxes below is correct, and at least one is incorrect. Identify which boxes are correct and which are incorrect. For each incorrect box, explain why it is incorrect.

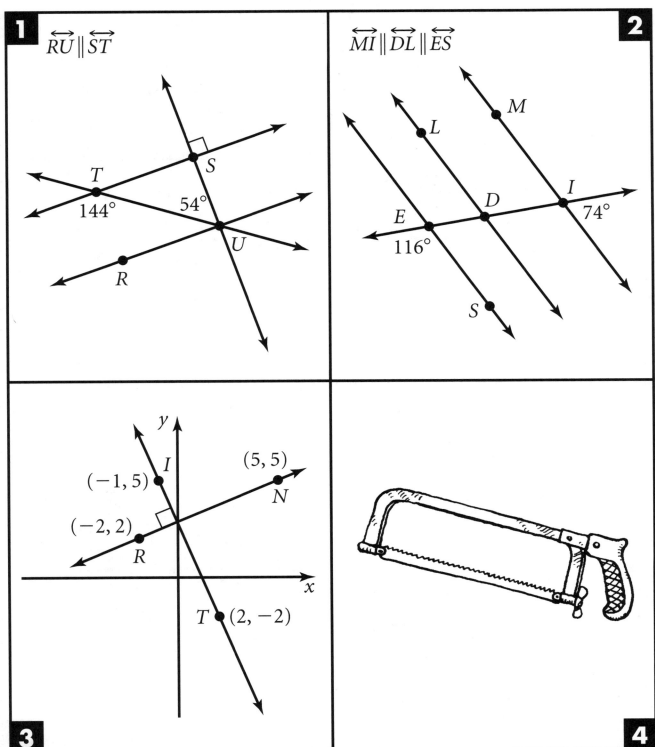

1 $\overleftrightarrow{RU} \parallel \overleftrightarrow{ST}$

$144°$ $54°$

2 $\overleftrightarrow{MI} \parallel \overleftrightarrow{DL} \parallel \overleftrightarrow{ES}$

$116°$ $74°$

3

$(-1, 5)$ I $(5, 5)$ N

$(-2, 2)$ R

T $(2, -2)$

4

What's Wrong with This Picture

Angle Properties and Parallel Properties

At least one of the boxes below is correct, and at least one is incorrect. Identify which boxes are correct and which are incorrect. For each incorrect box, explain why it is incorrect.

1

IF X = 6,
THEN X² = 36.

2

$\overleftrightarrow{DG} \parallel \overleftrightarrow{EF}$

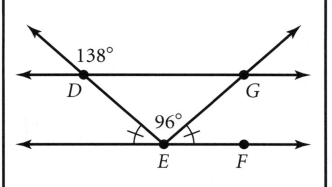

138°

D   G

96°

E   F

3

$\overleftrightarrow{SU} \parallel \overleftrightarrow{VE}$

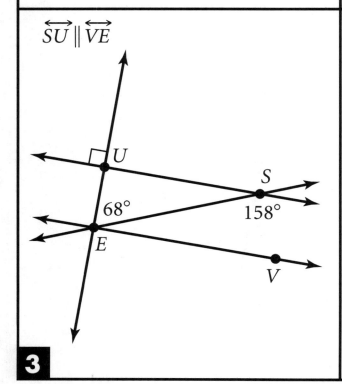

U

S

68°   158°

E

V

4

Slope $\overleftrightarrow{ME} = \frac{5}{8}$

Slope $\overleftrightarrow{KI} = \frac{5}{8}$

Slope $\overleftrightarrow{MI} = -\frac{8}{5}$

E

M   138°

K

I

What's Wrong with This Picture

Angle Properties and Parallel Properties

At least one of the boxes below is correct, and at least one is incorrect. Identify which boxes are correct and which are incorrect. For each incorrect box, explain why it is incorrect.

1

97°

83°

2

IF X² = 36,
THEN X = 6.

3

$\overleftrightarrow{AB} \parallel \overleftrightarrow{CD}, \overleftrightarrow{AC} \parallel \overleftrightarrow{BD}, \overleftrightarrow{CD} \parallel \overleftrightarrow{EF}$

108°
A   B

C   D

72°
E   F

4

71°

69°

What's Wrong with This Picture ❓ 9

At least one of the boxes below is correct, and at least one is incorrect. Identify which boxes are correct and which are incorrect. For each incorrect box, explain why it is incorrect.

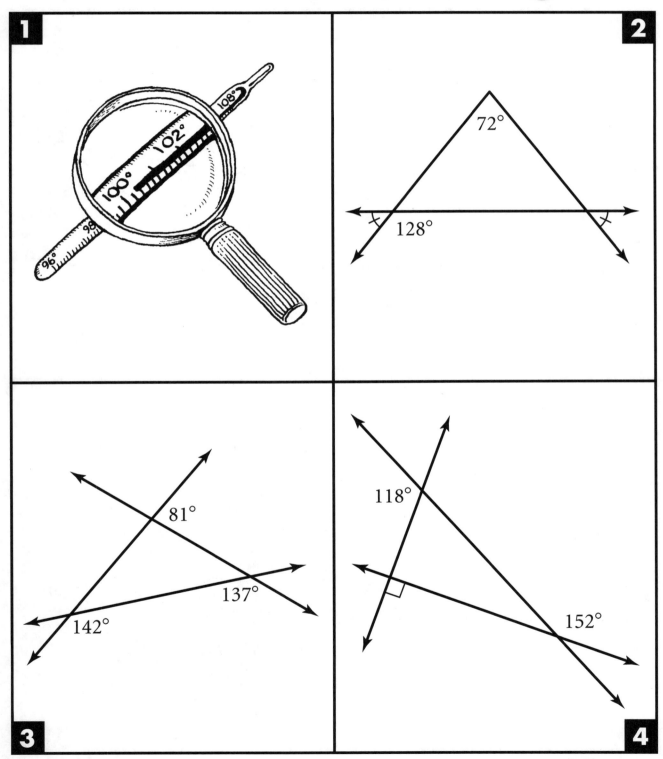

At least one of the boxes below is correct, and at least one is incorrect. Identify which boxes are correct and which are incorrect. For each incorrect box, explain why it is incorrect.

1

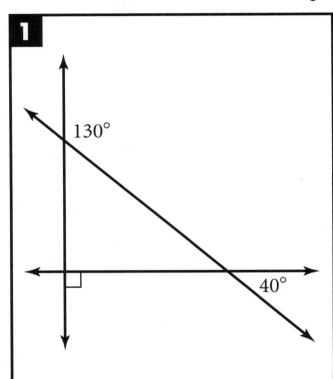

2

Slope $\overleftrightarrow{AB} = \frac{1}{6}$ Slope $\overleftrightarrow{AC} = -\frac{9}{7}$

Slope $\overleftrightarrow{DC} = \frac{1}{6}$ Slope $\overleftrightarrow{BD} = \frac{7}{9}$

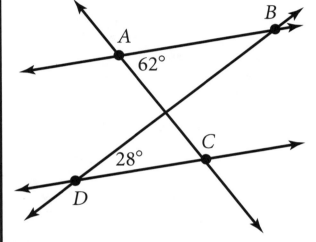

3

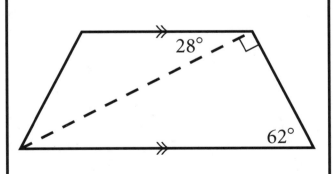

4

Postallog's Raisin Bran
(family style)
64 cm × 150 cm × 325 cm

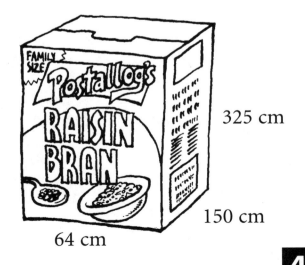

325 cm

150 cm

64 cm

What's Wrong with This Picture

Triangle Sum Properties, Third Angle, and Exterior Angle Properties

At least one of the boxes below is correct, and at least one is incorrect. Identify which boxes are correct and which are incorrect. For each incorrect box, explain why it is incorrect.

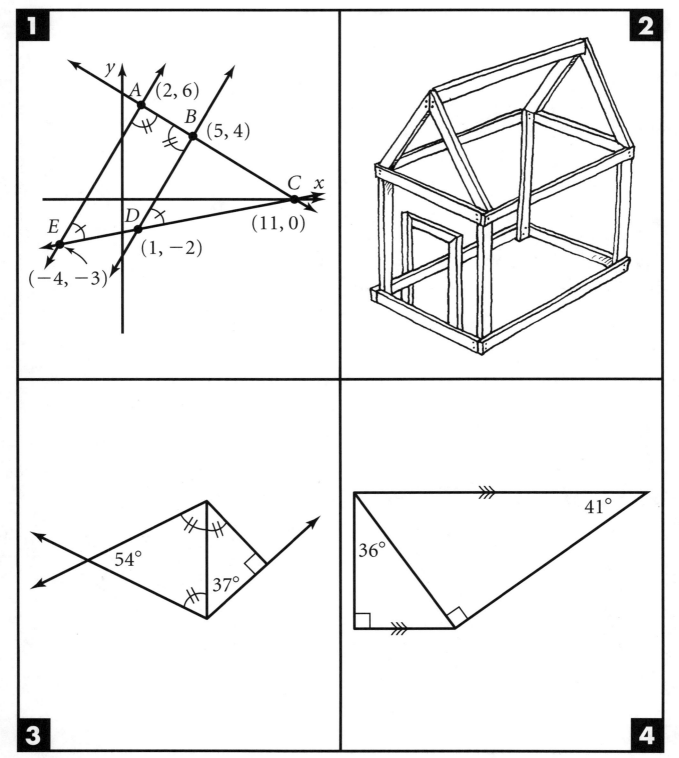

What's Wrong with This Picture

Triangle Sum Properties, Third Angle, and Exterior Angle Properties

At least one of the boxes below is correct, and at least one is incorrect. Identify which boxes are correct and which are incorrect. For each incorrect box, explain why it is incorrect.

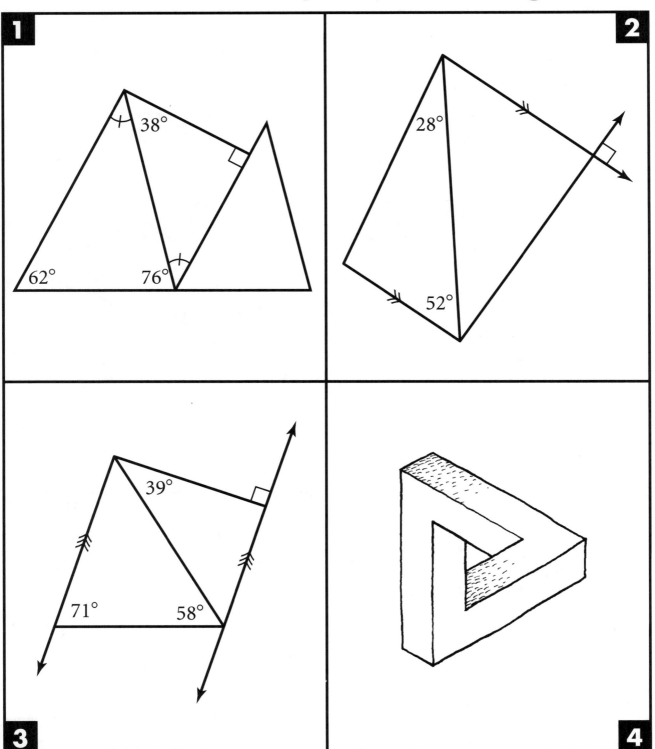

What's Wrong with This Picture

Parallel and Triangle Sum Properties and Isosceles Triangle Properties

At least one of the boxes below is correct, and at least one is incorrect. Identify which boxes are correct and which are incorrect. For each incorrect box, explain why it is incorrect.

1

48°

2

There are 365 and a quarter days in a year, so it must take slightly less than 30 years for a billion seconds to pass.

3

36°

104°

4

148°   116°

What's Wrong with This Picture

Parallel and Triangle Sum Properties and Isosceles Triangle Properties

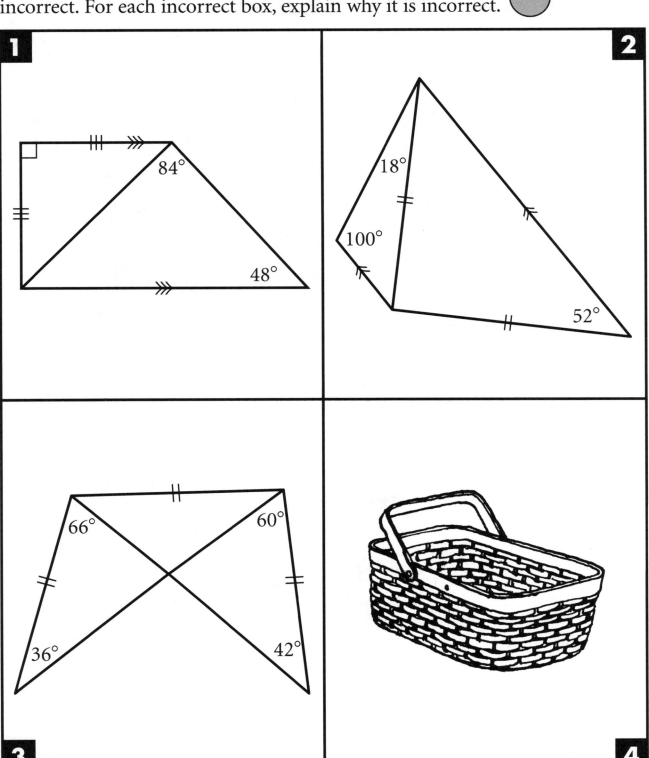

At least one of the boxes below is correct, and at least one is incorrect. Identify which boxes are correct and which are incorrect. For each incorrect box, explain why it is incorrect.

What's Wrong with This Picture

Parallel and Triangle Sum Properties and Isosceles Triangle Properties

At least one of the boxes below is correct, and at least one is incorrect. Identify which boxes are correct and which are incorrect. For each incorrect box, explain why it is incorrect.

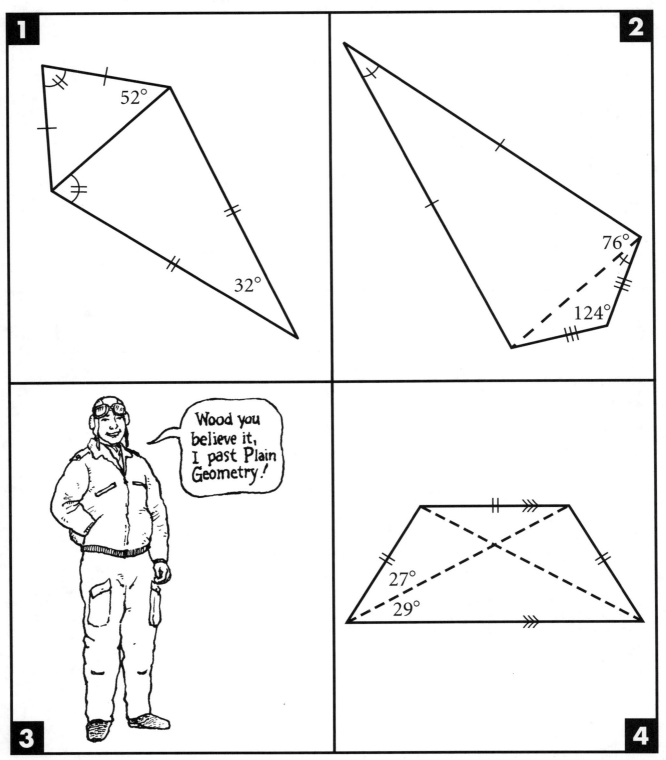

What's Wrong with This Picture

Parallel and Triangle Sum Properties and Isosceles Triangle Properties

At least one of the boxes below is correct, and at least one is incorrect. Identify which boxes are correct and which are incorrect. For each incorrect box, explain why it is incorrect.

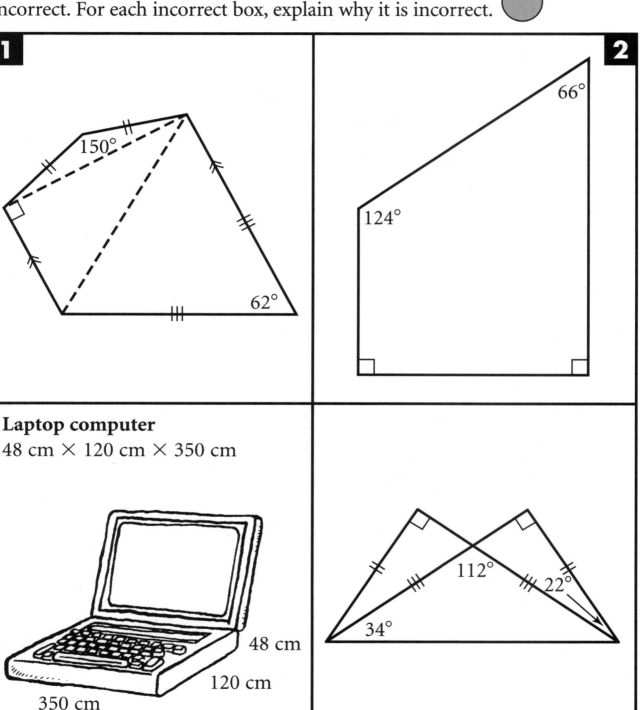

3 Laptop computer
48 cm × 120 cm × 350 cm

What's Wrong with This Picture

Polygon Sum Properties

At least one of the boxes below is correct, and at least one is incorrect. Identify which boxes are correct and which are incorrect. For each incorrect box, explain why it is incorrect.

At least one of the boxes below is correct, and at least one is incorrect. Identify which boxes are correct and which are incorrect. For each incorrect box, explain why it is incorrect.

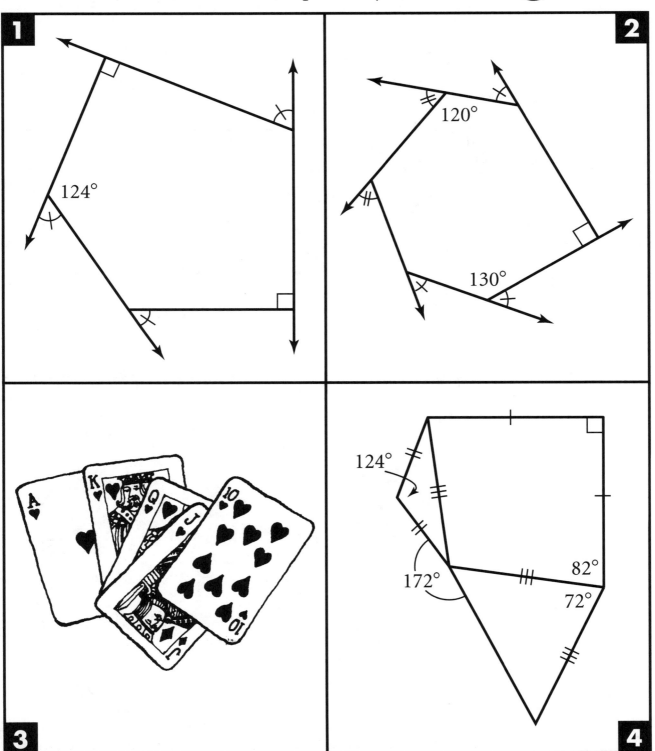

What's Wrong with This Picture

Polygon Sum Properties

19

At least one of the boxes below is correct, and at least one is incorrect. Identify which boxes are correct and which are incorrect. For each incorrect box, explain why it is incorrect.

1

68°

140° 38°

2

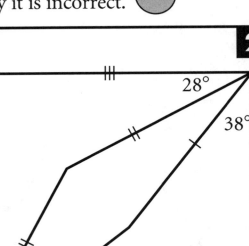

28°

38°

24°

3

Each pentagon is regular.
The hexagon is regular.

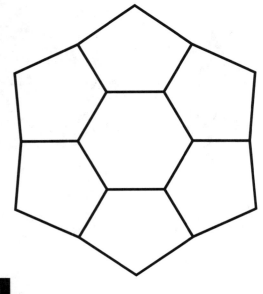

4

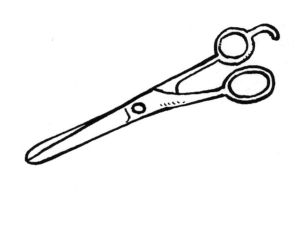

What's Wrong with This Picture

Polygon Sum Properties

At least one of the boxes below is correct, and at least one is incorrect. Identify which boxes are correct and which are incorrect. For each incorrect box, explain why it is incorrect.

1

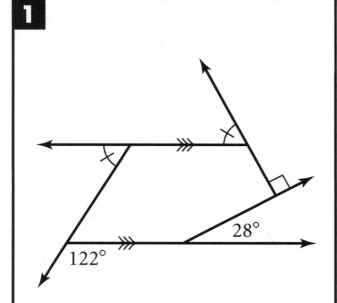

122°   28°

2

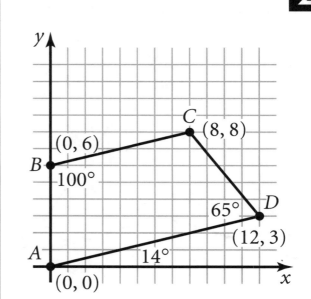

C (8, 8)

(0, 6) B

100°

65° D

(12, 3)

A

(0, 0)   14°

3

This arch is made up of nine isosceles trapezoids.

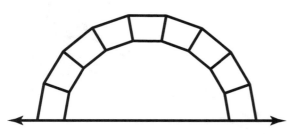

Each isosceles trapezoid has acute base angles of 80°.

4

What's Wrong with This Picture

Circle Properties

At least one of the boxes below is correct, and at least one is incorrect. Identify which boxes are correct and which are incorrect. For each incorrect box, explain why it is incorrect.

What's Wrong with This Picture

Circle Properties

At least one of the boxes below is correct, and at least one is incorrect. Identify which boxes are correct and which are incorrect. For each incorrect box, explain why it is incorrect.

1

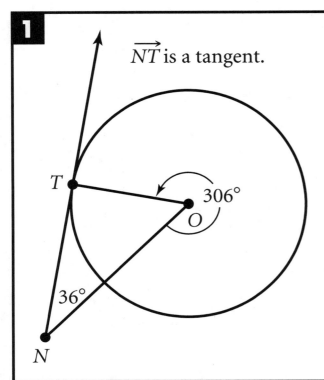

$\overrightarrow{NT}$ is a tangent.

2

$\overrightarrow{AR}$ and $\overrightarrow{AY}$ are tangents.

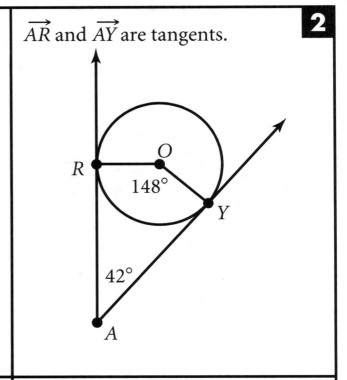

Problem

True or False?

For every real number x:

$$|x + 3| = x + 3$$

Solution

False

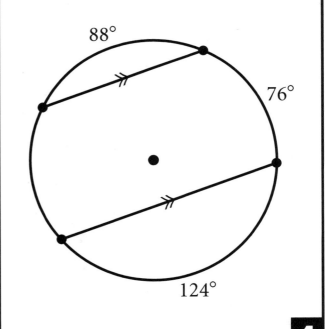

3

4

What's Wrong with This Picture

Circle Properties

At least one of the boxes below is correct, and at least one is incorrect. Identify which boxes are correct and which are incorrect. For each incorrect box, explain why it is incorrect.

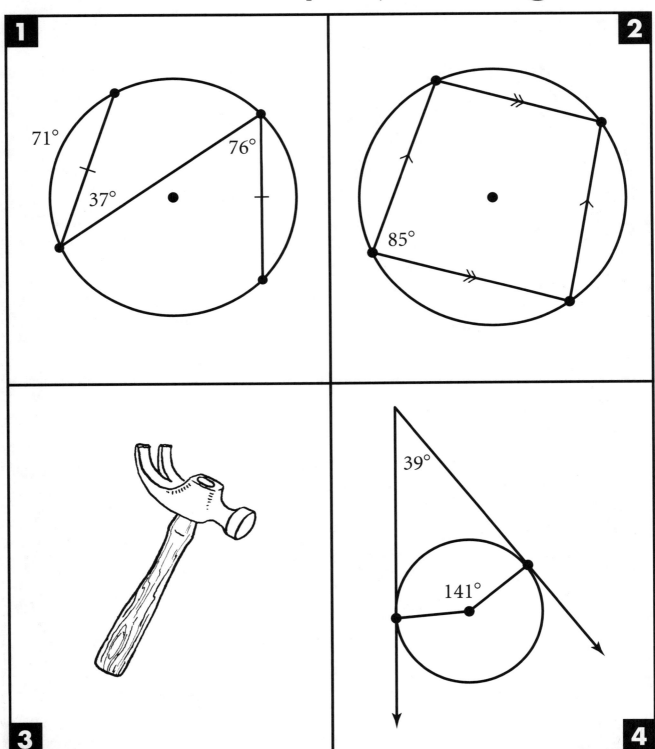

At least one of the boxes below is correct, and at least one is incorrect. Identify which boxes are correct and which are incorrect. For each incorrect box, explain why it is incorrect.

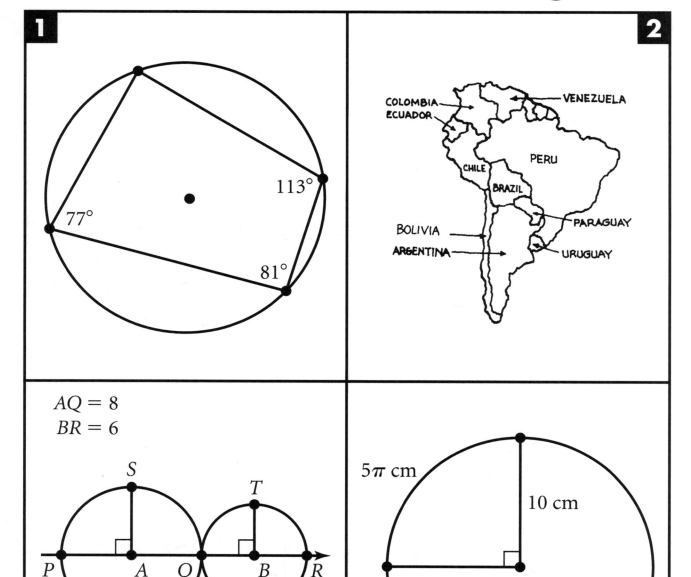

1

$113°$
$77°$
$81°$

2

COLOMBIA — VENEZUELA
ECUADOR
CHILE
PERU
BRAZIL
BOLIVIA
ARGENTINA
PARAGUAY
URUGUAY

3

$AQ = 8$
$BR = 6$

S
T
P   A   Q   B   R

$2m\widehat{SQ} = 3m\widehat{TR}$

4

5π cm
10 cm

What's Wrong with This Picture

Review

At least one of the boxes below is correct, and at least one is incorrect. Identify which boxes are correct and which are incorrect. For each incorrect box, explain why it is incorrect.

1

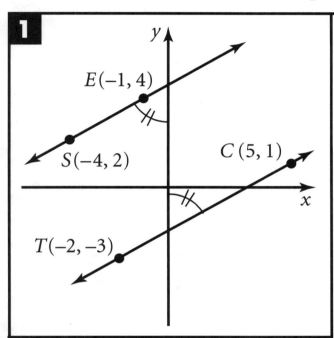

$E(-1, 4)$
$S(-4, 2)$
$C(5, 1)$
$T(-2, -3)$

2

All quadrilaterals are congruent rhombuses.

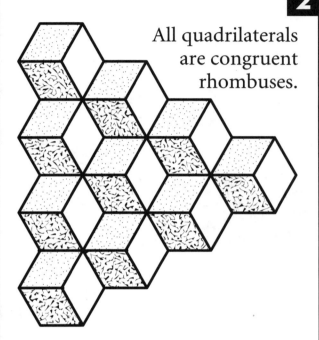

3

Perimeter of quadrilateral $PQRS = 68$

$AP = 10$ cm	$BQ = 6$ cm
$DS = 8$ cm	$QR = 16$ cm

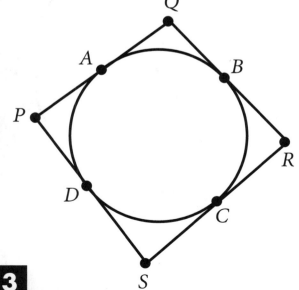

4

© 2003 Key Curriculum Press

What's Wrong with This Picture

Area Properties

At least one of the boxes below is correct, and at least one is incorrect. Identify which boxes are correct and which are incorrect. For each incorrect box, explain why it is incorrect.

1

2

Perimeter = 92 cm
Area = 504 cm²

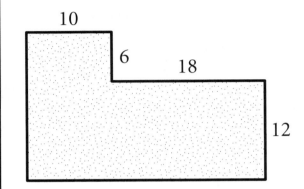

All lengths are in centimeters.

3

Area = 4800 cm²

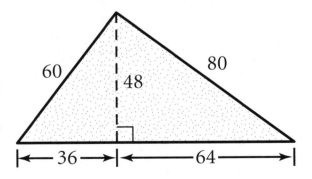

All lengths are in centimeters.

4

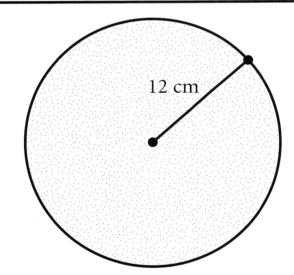

Circumference = 24π cm
Area = 144π cm²

26 • What's Wrong with This Picture?

© 2003 Key Curriculum Press

What's Wrong with This Picture

Area Properties

At least one of the boxes below is correct, and at least one is incorrect. Identify which boxes are correct and which are incorrect. For each incorrect box, explain why it is incorrect.

1

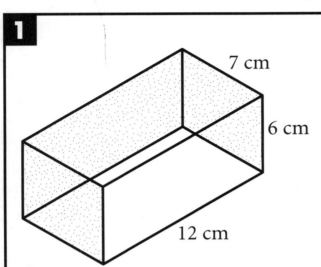

7 cm

6 cm

12 cm

The shaded surface area of the
6 cm × 7 cm × 12 cm box
is 114 cm².

2

3

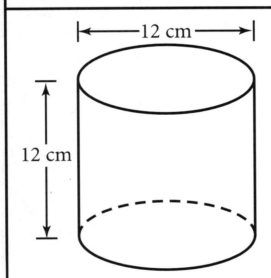

|←——— 12 cm ———→|

12 cm

The total surface area of the
cylinder is 216π cm².

4

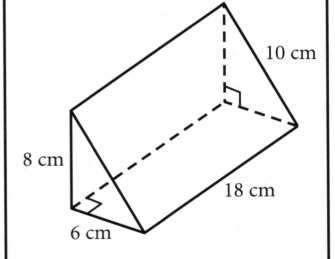

10 cm

8 cm

18 cm

6 cm

The total surface area of the
five faces of the right triangular
prism is 300 cm².

What's Wrong with This Picture

Area Properties

At least one of the boxes below is correct, and at least one is incorrect. Identify which boxes are correct and which are incorrect. For each incorrect box, explain why it is incorrect.

1

Perimeter = 98 cm
Area = 544 cm^2

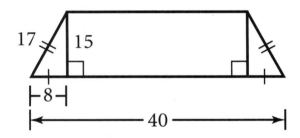

2

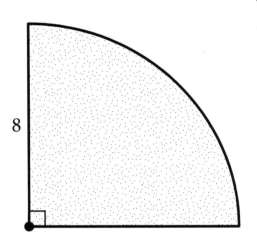

8

Perimeter = $(16 + 4\pi)$ cm
Area = 64π cm^2

3

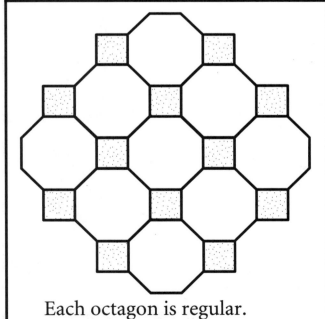

Each octagon is regular.
Each quadrilateral is regular.

4

12

Area of rectangle = 96 cm^2
Perimeter of rectangle = 40 cm
Shaded area = 52π cm^2

What's Wrong with This Picture

At least one of the boxes below is correct, and at least one is incorrect. Identify which boxes are correct and which are incorrect. For each incorrect box, explain why it is incorrect.

1

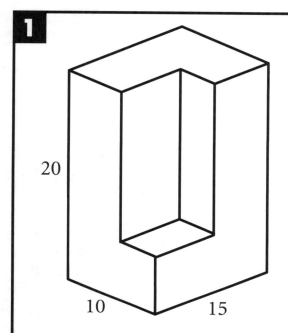

Total surface area = 1300 cm²

2

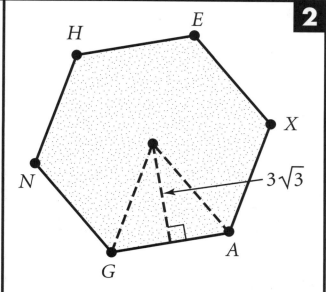

HEXAGN is a regular hexagon.
Perimeter = 72 cm
Area = 384 √3 cm²

3

4

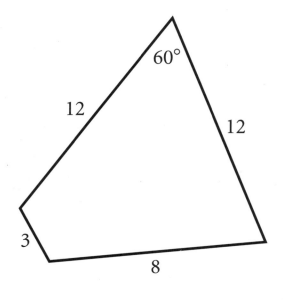

What's Wrong with This Picture

Pythagorean Theorem

At least one of the boxes below is correct, and at least one is incorrect. Identify which boxes are correct and which are incorrect. For each incorrect box, explain why it is incorrect.

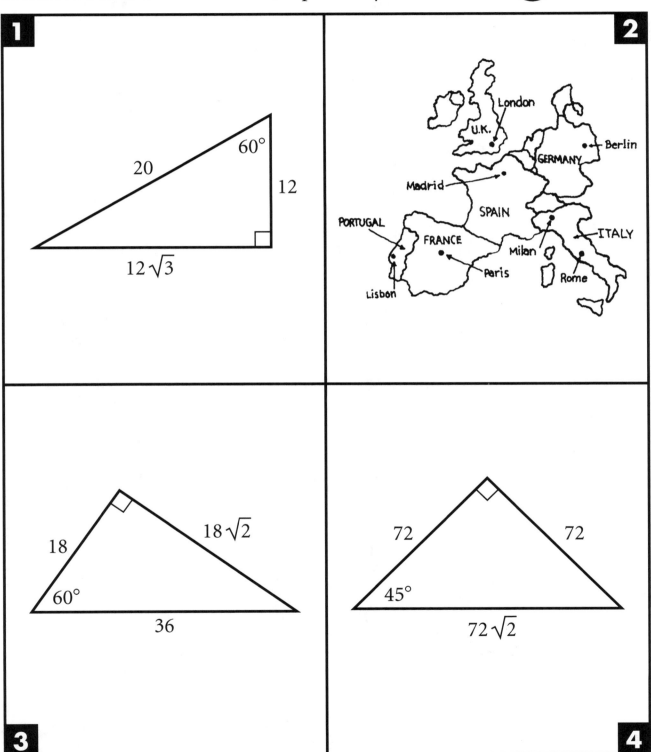

At least one of the boxes below is correct, and at least one is incorrect. Identify which boxes are correct and which are incorrect. For each incorrect box, explain why it is incorrect.

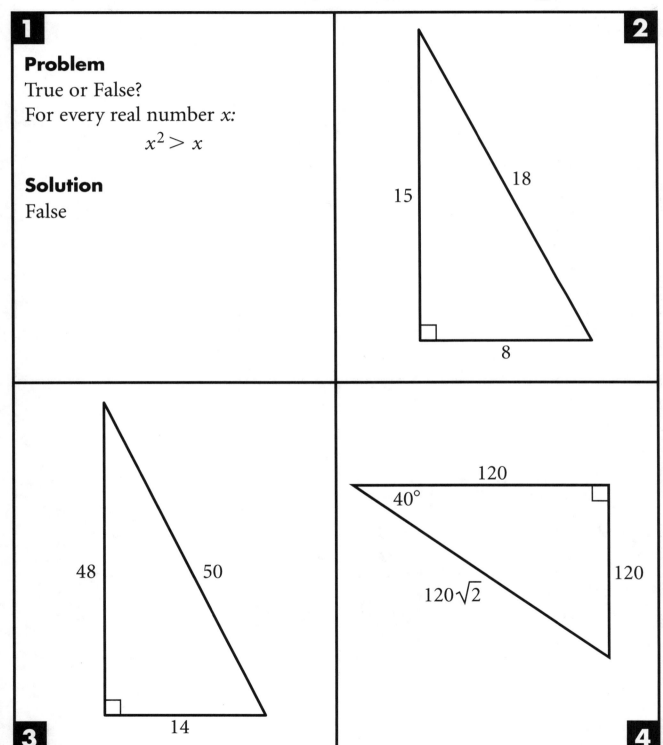

1

Problem

True or False?

For every real number x:
$$x^2 > x$$

Solution

False

2

15   18

8

3

48   50

14

4

120

40°

120√2   120

What's Wrong with This Picture

Pythagorean Theorem

At least one of the boxes below is correct, and at least one is incorrect. Identify which boxes are correct and which are incorrect. For each incorrect box, explain why it is incorrect.

1

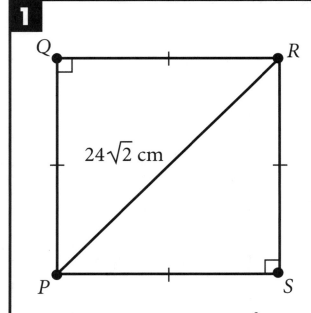

Area($PQRS$) = 576 cm^2
Perimeter($PQRS$) = 48 cm

2

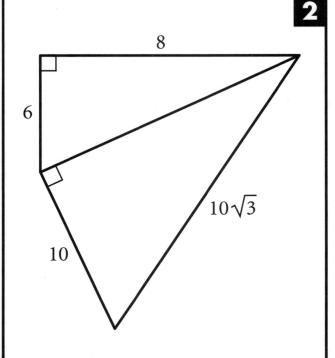

3

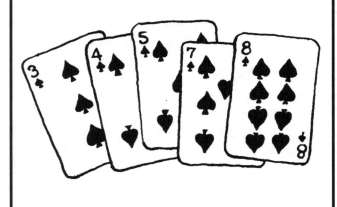

4

What's Wrong with This Picture

Pythagorean Theorem

At least one of the boxes below is correct, and at least one is incorrect. Identify which boxes are correct and which are incorrect. For each incorrect box, explain why it is incorrect.

1

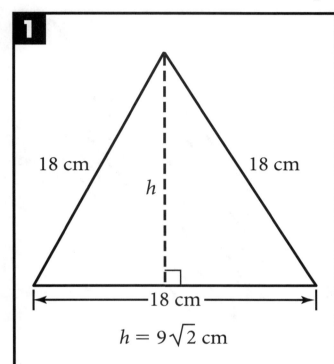

18 cm   18 cm

h

18 cm

$h = 9\sqrt{2}$ cm

2

3

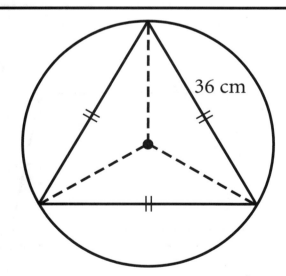

36 cm

Area of circle = 432π cm^2

Area of equilateral triangle = $324\sqrt{3}$ cm^2

4

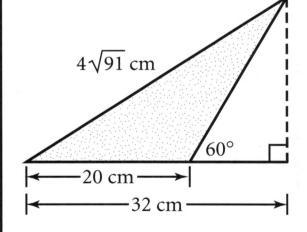

$4\sqrt{91}$ cm

60°

20 cm

32 cm

Area of shaded triangle = $120\sqrt{3}$ cm^2

Perimeter of shaded triangle = $\left(44 + 4\sqrt{91}\right)$ cm

What's Wrong with This Picture

Pythagorean Theorem

At least one of the boxes below is correct, and at least one is incorrect. Identify which boxes are correct and which are incorrect. For each incorrect box, explain why it is incorrect.

1

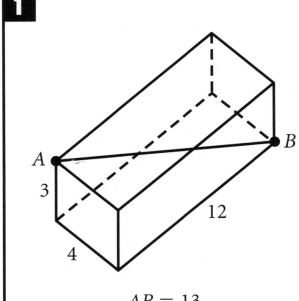

$AB = 13$

2

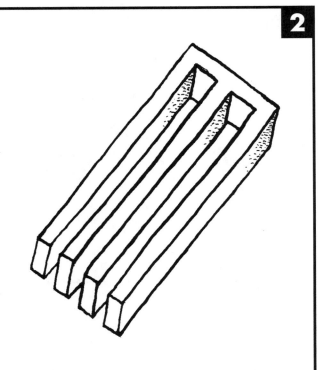

3

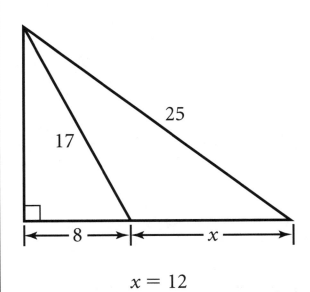

$x = 12$

4

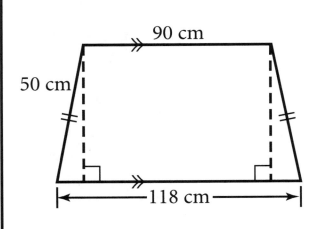

90 cm

50 cm

118 cm

Area of trapezoid = 392 cm^2

At least one of the boxes below is correct, and at least one is incorrect. Identify which boxes are correct and which are incorrect. For each incorrect box, explain why it is incorrect.

1

Wear is he now? I'm board waiting.

2

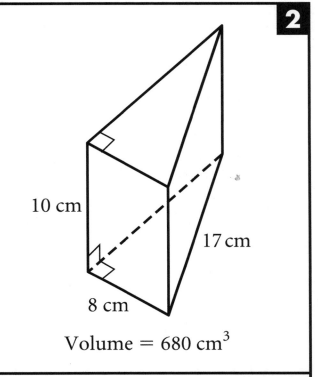

10 cm

17 cm

8 cm

Volume = 680 cm³

3

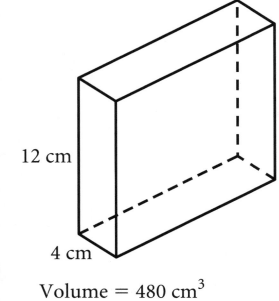

12 cm

4 cm

Volume = 480 cm³
Total surface area = 416 cm²

4

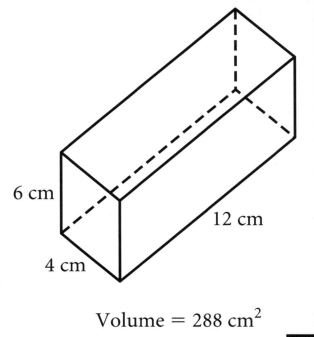

6 cm

12 cm

4 cm

Volume = 288 cm²

What's Wrong with This Picture

Volume

At least one of the boxes below is correct, and at least one is incorrect. Identify which boxes are correct and which are incorrect. For each incorrect box, explain why it is incorrect.

1

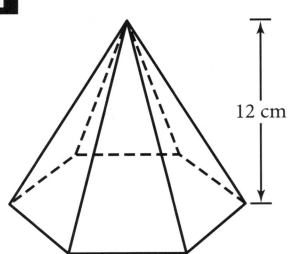

12 cm

Area of base = 210 cm^2
Volume of pyramid = 1260 cm^3

2

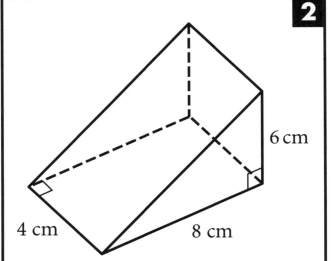

6 cm

4 cm   8 cm

Total surface area = 96 cm^2
Volume = 96 cm^3

3

Problem
True or False?
$(\sqrt{3} - \sqrt{2})(\sqrt{3} + \sqrt{2}) = 1$

Solution
True

4

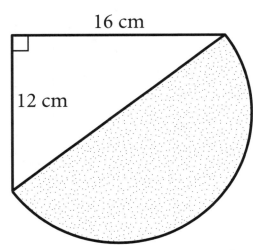

16 cm

12 cm

Shaded area = 100π cm^2

What's Wrong with This Picture

Volume

At least one of the boxes below is correct, and at least one is incorrect. Identify which boxes are correct and which are incorrect. For each incorrect box, explain why it is incorrect.

1

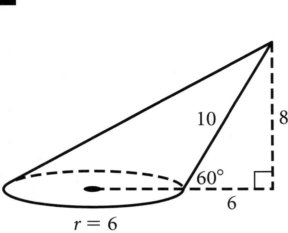

Volume = 96π cm^3
All lengths are in centimeters.

2

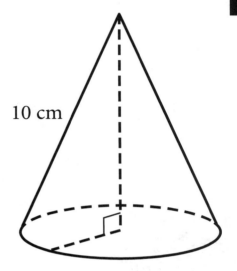

Area of base = 36π cm^2
Volume of cone = 96π cm^3

3

4

Volume = 152 cm^3
$H = 2$ cm

What's Wrong with This Picture

38

At least one of the boxes below is correct, and at least one is incorrect. Identify which boxes are correct and which are incorrect. For each incorrect box, explain why it is incorrect.

1

2

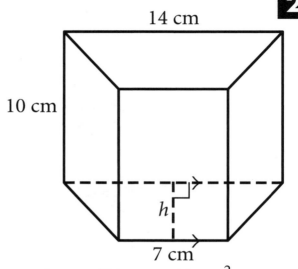

Area of base = 42 cm^2
Volume of prism = 420 cm^3
h = 4 cm

3

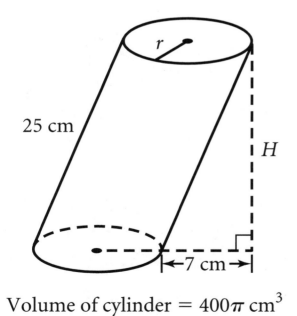

Volume of cylinder = 400π cm^3
r = 4 cm

All lengths are in centimeters.

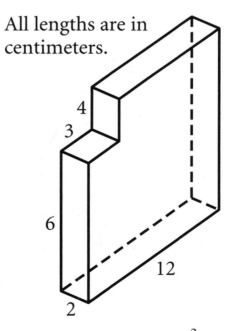

Volume = 240 cm^3

4

What's Wrong with This Picture

At least one of the boxes below is correct, and at least one is incorrect. Identify which boxes are correct and which are incorrect. For each incorrect box, explain why it is incorrect.

1

$\overleftrightarrow{AB} \parallel \overleftrightarrow{CD}$

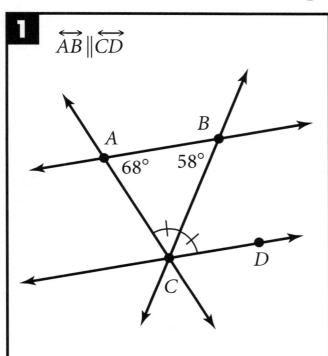

2

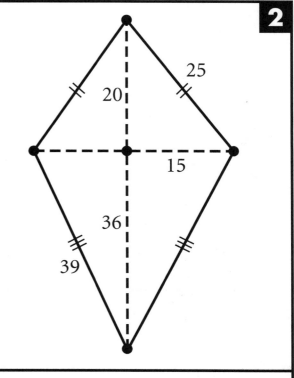

3

4

Problem

A regular octagon has all of its diagonals drawn. What is the probability of randomly selecting one of the shortest diagonals from all of the diagonals?

Solution

Because there are 20 diagonals in an octagon and there are 8 short diagonals, the probability is $\frac{2}{5}$, or 40%.

What's Wrong with This Picture

Similarity

At least one of the boxes below is correct, and at least one is incorrect. Identify which boxes are correct and which are incorrect. For each incorrect box, explain why it is incorrect.

1

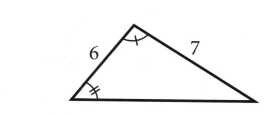

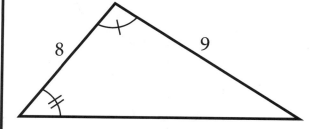

2

Problem

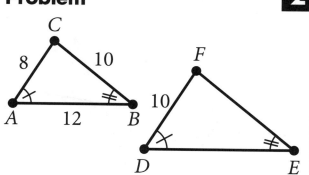

Find the perimeter of $\triangle DEF$.

Solution

$$\frac{\text{side } \triangle ABC}{\text{side } \triangle DEF} = \frac{\text{perimeter } \triangle ABC}{\text{perimeter } \triangle DEF}$$

$$\frac{8}{10} = \frac{30}{P}$$

$$P = 37.5$$

3

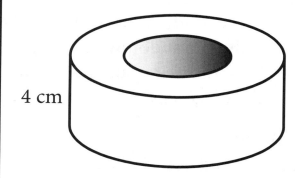

4 cm

Small diameter = 6 cm
Large diameter = 12 cm
Volume = 108π cm^3

4

What's Wrong with This Picture? 41

Similarity

At least one of the boxes below is correct, and at least one is incorrect. Identify which boxes are correct and which are incorrect. For each incorrect box, explain why it is incorrect.

1

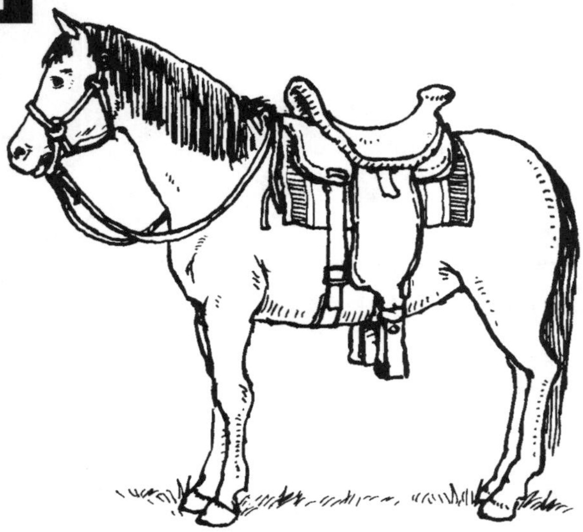

2

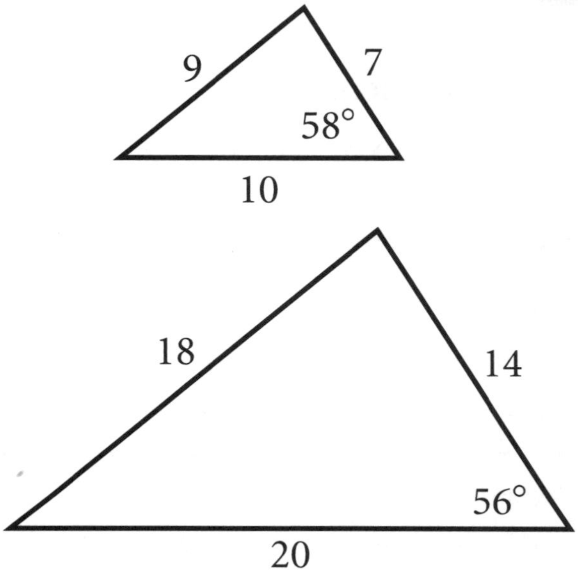

3

Problem

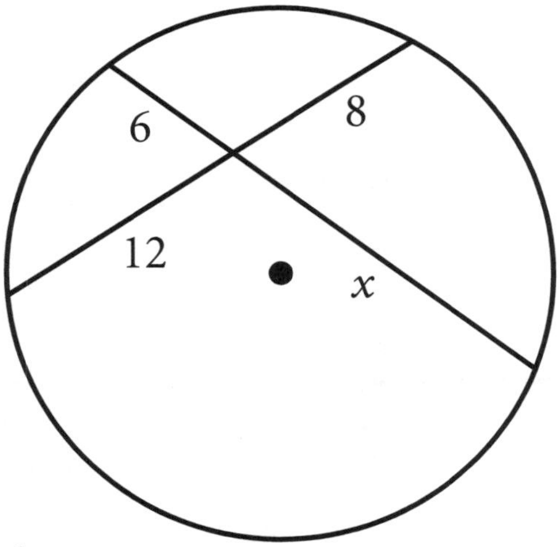

Find x.

Solution

$$\frac{6}{8} = \frac{12}{x}$$
$$6x = 84$$
$$x = 14$$

4

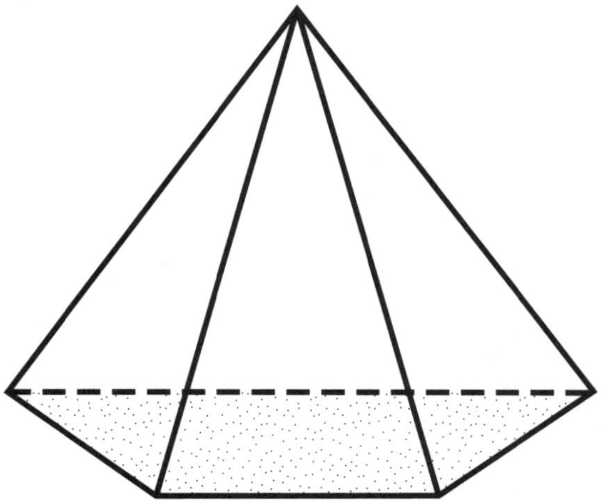

Area of base = 120 cm^2

Volume of pyramid = 720 cm^3

H = 18 cm

At least one of the boxes below is correct, and at least one is incorrect. Identify which boxes are correct and which are incorrect. For each incorrect box, explain why it is incorrect.

1

Problem

Solve the inequality.

$$3x + 7 \leq 13$$

Solution

$$3x + 7 \leq 13$$
$$3x \geq 6$$
$$x \geq 2$$

Problem

$\triangle BIG \sim \triangle SML$, $SL = 26$, $BG = 39$
Area of $\triangle BIG = 648$ cm^2
Find A, the area of $\triangle SML$.

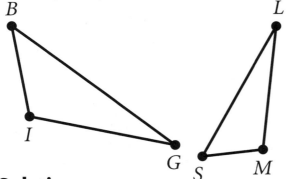

Solution

$$\left(\frac{26}{39}\right)^2 = \frac{\text{area } \triangle SML}{\text{area } \triangle BIG}$$

$$\left(\frac{2}{3}\right)^2 = \frac{\text{area } \triangle SML}{648}$$

$$9A = 2592$$

3 $$A = 288 \text{ cm}^2$$

Problem   **2**

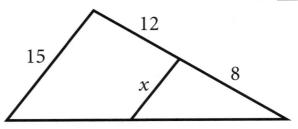

Find x.

Solution

$$\frac{8}{12} = \frac{x}{15}$$

$$x = 10$$

Problem

Rectangle *RECT* is similar to rectangle *ANGL*.

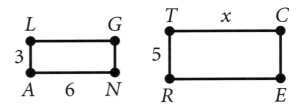

Find A, the area of *RECT*.

Solution

$$\frac{3}{5} = \frac{18}{A}$$

$$3A = 90$$

$$A = 30$$ **4**

What's Wrong with This Picture

Trigonometry

At least one of the boxes below is correct, and at least one is incorrect. Identify which boxes are correct and which are incorrect. For each incorrect box, explain why it is incorrect.

---

1 Problem

Cylinders A and B are similar.
$R = 12$ cm, $H = 60$ cm
$r = 4$ cm, $h = 20$ cm

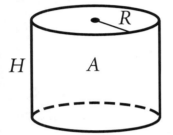 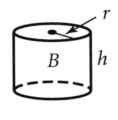

Find the ratio $\dfrac{\text{volume } B}{\text{volume } A}$

Solution

$$\frac{\text{volume } B}{\text{volume } A} = \left(\frac{4}{12}\right)^3 \Rightarrow$$

$$\frac{\text{volume } B}{\text{volume } A} = \frac{1}{27}$$

2

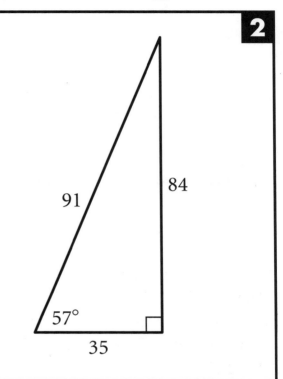

3

4

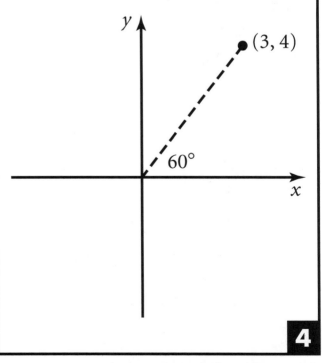

At least one of the boxes below is correct, and at least one is incorrect. Identify which boxes are correct and which are incorrect. For each incorrect box, explain why it is incorrect.

1

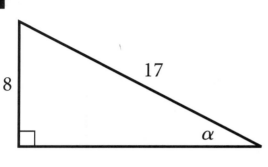

$$\sin \alpha = \frac{8}{17}$$

$$\cos \alpha = \frac{15}{17}$$

$$\tan \alpha = \frac{8}{15}$$

Problem

Find x to the nearest whole number.

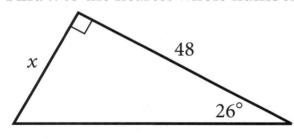

Solution

$$\sin 26° = \frac{x}{48}$$

$$x = 48 \sin 26°$$

$$x = 21$$

Problem **2**

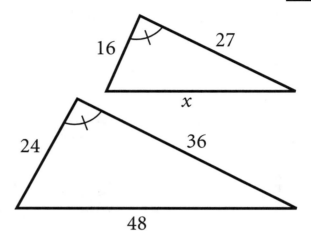

Find x.

Solution

$$\frac{36}{48} = \frac{27}{x}$$

$$36x = 1296$$

$$x = 36$$

3   **4**

At least one of the boxes below is correct, and at least one is incorrect. Identify which boxes are correct and which are incorrect. For each incorrect box, explain why it is incorrect.

1

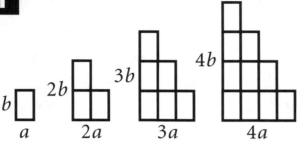

Problem

If the pattern continues, write the expression for the area of the tenth shape in the block pattern.

Solution

The area is $55ab$.

2

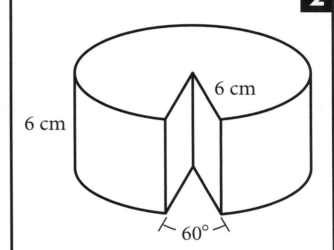

Volume $= 180\pi$ cm^3

Problem

$\overline{CD}$ is the bisector of $\angle C$. Find x.

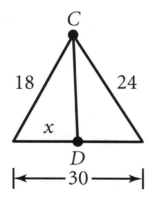

Solution

Because $\overline{CD}$ is the bisector of $\angle C$,

$$x = \frac{1}{2}(30)$$
$$x = 15$$

3

Problem

Find the height of the cone, accurate to one decimal place.

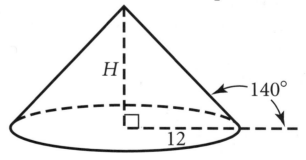

Solution

$$\tan 40° = \frac{H}{12}$$
$$H = 12 \tan 40°$$
$$H = 10.1$$

4

At least one of the boxes below is correct, and at least one is incorrect. Identify which boxes are correct and which are incorrect. For each incorrect box, explain why it is incorrect.

---

1 Problem

Find the equation of the median $\overline{BD}$ in $\triangle ABC$ with vertices $A(-4, 0)$, $B(6, 0)$, and $C(0, 8)$

Solution

The coordinates of D: $(-2, 4)$.

Slope of $\overline{BD} = \dfrac{4 - 0}{-2 - 6} = -\dfrac{1}{2}$,

therefore $y = -\dfrac{1}{2}x + b$. Or

$0 = -\dfrac{1}{2}(6) + b$, thus $b = 3$.

$$\therefore y = -\dfrac{1}{2}x + 3$$

Problem 2

Find the equation of the line through the altitude $\overline{AD}$ in $\triangle ABC$ with vertices $A(-2, 0)$, $B(6, 0)$, and $C(0, 8)$.

Solution

The coordinates of D: $(3, 4)$.

Slope of $\overline{BC} = \dfrac{8 - 0}{0 - 6} = -\dfrac{4}{3}$,

therefore the slope of $\overline{AD} = \dfrac{3}{4}$

So $y = \dfrac{3}{4}x + b$

or $4 = \dfrac{3}{4}(3) + b$, so $b = \dfrac{7}{4}$

$$\therefore 4y - 3x = 7$$

---

3 Problem

Find the area, to the nearest square centimeter, of a regular pentagon with each side measuring 24 cm.

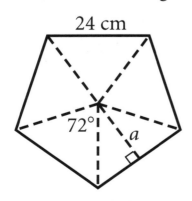

24 cm

72°

a

Solution

$$\tan 72° = \frac{12}{a}$$

$$a = \frac{12}{\tan 72°}$$

$$A = \frac{1}{2}ap$$

$$A = \frac{1}{2}\left(\frac{12}{\tan 72°}\right)(24 \cdot 5)$$

$$A = 234 \text{ cm}^2$$

What's Wrong with This Picture

Transformational Geometry

At least one of the boxes below is correct, and at least one is incorrect. Identify which boxes are correct and which are incorrect. For each incorrect box, explain why it is incorrect.

1

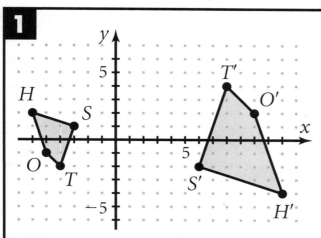

Problem

What is the coordinate rule $[(x, y) \rightarrow (?, ?)]$ that transforms polygon HOTS to H'O'T'S'?

Solution

$(x, y) \rightarrow (-2x, -2y)$

3

Perimeter = 74 cm

Area = 312 cm^2

24 cm

12 cm

13 cm

2

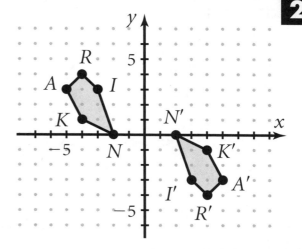

K'A'R'I'N' is the image polygon of KARIN using the transformational rule $(x, y) \rightarrow (-x, -y)$.

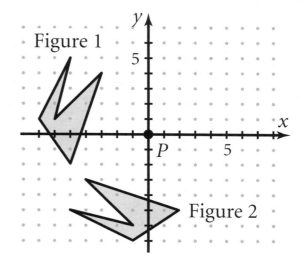

Figure 1 was rotated 270° clockwise about the center of rotation, P, to get Figure 2.

4

At least one of the boxes below is correct, and at least one is incorrect. Identify which boxes are correct and which are incorrect. For each incorrect box, explain why it is incorrect.

---

1 Proof that a pound is equivalent to 256 ounces:

$$2 \text{ pounds} = 32 \text{ ounces}$$

$$\tfrac{1}{2} \text{ pound} = 8 \text{ ounces}$$

(multiplying equals by equals)

$$1 \text{ pound} = 256 \text{ ounces}$$

Conjecture

The midpoint of the hypotenuse of a right triangle is equally distant from all three vertices.

Proof

Given right triangle ABC with $\overline{AB}$ the hypotenuse. Select vertices $A(2a, 0)$, $B(0, 2b)$, and $C(0, 0)$. Then the midpoint of $\overline{AB}$ is M (a, b) and thus

$$MA = \sqrt{(2a - a)^2 + (b - 0)^2}$$

$$= \sqrt{a^2 + b^2}$$

$$MB = \sqrt{(a - 0)^2 + (2b - b)^2}$$

$$= \sqrt{a^2 + b^2}$$

$$MC = \sqrt{(a - 0)^2 + (b - 0)^2}$$

$$= \sqrt{a^2 + b^2}$$

3

Conjecture **2**

The median to the base of an isosceles triangle is also the angle bisector of the vertex angle.

Proof

Given $\triangle ABC$ with $\overline{AC} \cong \overline{BC}$, and $\overline{CD}$ a median.

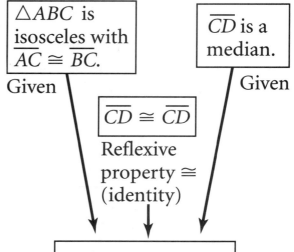

What's Wrong with This Picture

Proof

At least one of the boxes below is correct, and at least one is incorrect. Identify which boxes are correct and which are incorrect. For each incorrect box, explain why it is incorrect.

---

1 **Conjecture**

If two segments bisect each other, then their endpoints form the vertices of a parallelogram.

Proof

Let $\overline{AB}$ and $\overline{CD}$ bisect each other at M. Then M is the midpoint of both $\overline{AB}$ and $\overline{CD}$, and thus $\overline{AM} \cong \overline{MB}$ and $\overline{CM} \cong \overline{MD}$. $\angle AMD \cong \angle BMC$ and $\angle AMC \cong \angle BMD$ because they are vertical angles. Thus $\triangle AMD \cong \triangle BMC$ and $\triangle AMC \cong \triangle BMD$ by SAS congruence shortcut. Thus $\angle DAM \cong \angle CBM$ and $\angle BDM \cong \angle ACM$ (CPCTC). Because the angles are congruent and they are alternate interior angles, $\overleftrightarrow{AD} \parallel \overleftrightarrow{BC}$ and $\overleftrightarrow{AC} \parallel \overleftrightarrow{BD}$. Because the opposite sides of quadrilateral $ACBD$ are parallel, $ACBD$ is a parallelogram.

Conjecture

If $a + b = x$ and $c + d = x$ and $a = c$, then $b = d$.

Proof

$a + b = x$	Given
$c + d = x$	Given
$a + b = c + d$	Substitution
$a = c$	Given
$\therefore b = d$	

Subtraction property of equality

2

3

What's Wrong with This Picture

Proof

At least one of the boxes below is correct, and at least one is incorrect. Identify which boxes are correct and which are incorrect. For each incorrect box, explain why it is incorrect.

1 Conjecture

There are two perpendiculars from a point to a line.

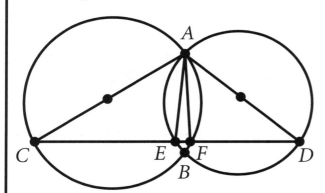

Proof

Given two circles intersecting at A and B. Draw diameters $\overline{AC}$ and $\overline{AD}$. Draw $\overline{CD}$. Label the points where $\overline{CD}$ intersects the circles E and F. Because $\angle CFA$ and $\angle DEA$ are each inscribed in a semicircle they must be right angles. Thus $\overline{AE}$ and $\overline{AF}$ are both perpendicular to $\overline{CD}$.

Conjecture 2

The sum of the measures of the five angles at the points of the 5-point-star polygon *STARY* is 180°.

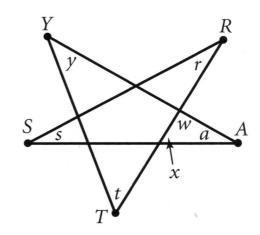

Proof

$x = s + r, w = t + y$
       Exterior angle theorem
$x + w + a = 180°$
       Triangle Sum theorem
$\therefore s + t + a + r + y = 180°$

Problem

Segment $\overline{FR}$ has two trisection points O, U. What is the probability of randomly selecting a point on $\overline{FR}$ that is closer to either of the endpoints than it is to one of the two trisection points?

Solution

The probability is $\frac{1}{3}$.

3

Solutions

Exercise 1

1. Incorrect. $118° + 72° \neq 180°$.
2. Correct. $1{,}000{,}000 \text{ sec} \cdot \frac{1 \text{ min}}{60 \text{ sec}} \cdot \frac{1 \text{ hr}}{60 \text{ min}} \cdot \frac{1 \text{ day}}{24 \text{ hr}} \approx 11.57$ days.
3. Correct. $48° + 42° = 90°$.
4. Incorrect. $m\angle AEC$ should equal $m\angle BED$ (vertical angles).

Exercise 2

1. Incorrect. $m\angle DEA + m\angle AEB = m\angle DEA + m\angle CEG = 38° + 54° = 92° \neq 90°$.
2. Correct. $m\angle APF + m\angle FPD + m\angle DPB = m\angle APF + m\angle EPC + m\angle DPB = 58° + 49° + 73° = 180°$.
3. Correct. Nothing in the marked diagram is incorrect or contradicts other information.
4. Incorrect. There are three pedals.

Exercise 3

1. Incorrect. $m\angle PXQ + m\angle QXR = m\angle RXS + m\angle QXR = m\angle VXW + m\angle QXR = 26° + 54° = 80° \neq 90°$.
2. Correct. $m\angle PQT + m\angle TQS + m\angle SQR = 74° + 90° + 16° = 180°$.
3. Incorrect. $m\angle AFB + m\angle BFC + m\angle CFD + m\angle DFE = m\angle DFE + m\angle BFC + m\angle BFC + m\angle DFE = 36° + 52° + 52° + 36° = 176° \neq 180°$.
4. Incorrect. Colorado and Wyoming are switched, and Arizona and New Mexico are switched.

Exercise 4

1. Correct. $m\angle EHF + m\angle FHG = m\angle EHF + m\angle GHA = m\angle EHF + m\angle CHD = 69° + 21° = 90°$.
2. Incorrect. $m\angle EKF + m\angle FKG = m\angle IKJ + m\angle FKG = 68° + 19° = 87° \neq 90°$.
3. Incorrect. $1999^2 - 1998^2 = 3997$ whereas $\frac{49^2 - 48^2}{49 + 48} = 1$, so the solution should be "False."
4. Incorrect. $m\angle RZS + m\angle SZT + m\angle TZU + m\angle UZV = m\angle RZS + m\angle SZT + m\angle SZT + m\angle UZV = m\angle RZS + m\angle WZX + m\angle WZX + m\angle UZV = 88° + 26° + 26° + 38° = 178° \neq 180°$.

Exercise 5

1. Incorrect. The two angle measures should be equal (alternate exterior angles).
2. Incorrect. Nashville and Louisville are switched, as are New Orleans and Little Rock.
3. Incorrect. Around H and K the angles are 82°, 98°, 82°, and 98°, which add to 360° (or 180° for any two consecutive angles), which is correct, but around I and L they are 72°, 98°, 72°, and 98°, which only add to 340° (or 170° for any two consecutive angles).
4. Correct. Slope of top $= \frac{2-1}{2-(-2)} = \frac{1}{4} = \frac{1-0}{4-0} =$ Slope of bottom.

Exercise 6

1. Correct. Around T the angles are 144°, 36°, 144°, and 36°, which add to 360° (or 180° for any two consecutive angles). Around S they are all 90°. Around U they are (clockwise) 54°, 90°, 36°, 54°, 90°, and 36°, which add to 360° (or 180° for any three consecutive angles). And inside $\triangle STU$ they are 90°, 36°, and 54°, which add to 180°.
2. Incorrect. By Alternate Interior Angles, Alternate Exterior Angles, and Corresponding Angles, the angles around each of E, D, and I would be 116°, 74°, 116°, and 74°, which would add to 380° (or 190° for any two consecutive angles).
3. Correct.
   Slope of $\overleftrightarrow{RN} = \frac{5-2}{5-(-2)} = \frac{3}{7}$,
   Slope of $\overleftrightarrow{IT} = \frac{-2-5}{2-(-1)} = -\frac{7}{3}$,
   $\frac{3}{7} \cdot \left(-\frac{7}{3}\right) = -1$
4. Incorrect. The saw blade is inverted.

Exercise 7

1. Correct.
2. Correct. The two equal angles at E are
   $$\frac{180° - 96°}{2} = 42°$$
   So by Alternate Interior Angles, Vertical

Angles, and Supplementary Angles, the angles around both D and G are 138°, 42°, 138°, and 42°, which add to 360° (or 180° for any two consecutive angles).

3. Correct. By Supplementary Angles, the smaller angles at S are 22°, so by Alternate Interior Angles (or Corresponding Angles) $m\angle SEV = 22°$. Then $m\angle UES + m\angle SEV = 68° + 22° = 90°$, which agrees with $\overleftrightarrow{UE} \perp \overleftrightarrow{VE}$ (because $\overleftrightarrow{UE} \perp \overleftrightarrow{SU}$ and $\overleftrightarrow{SU} \parallel \overleftrightarrow{VE}$).

4. Incorrect. The slopes imply that $\overleftrightarrow{ME} \parallel \overleftrightarrow{KI}$, $\overleftrightarrow{MI} \perp \overleftrightarrow{ME}$, and $\overleftrightarrow{MI} \perp \overleftrightarrow{KI}$. By Consecutive Interior Angles, $m\angle EMK = 180° - 138° = 42°$. But then $m\angle EMK + m\angle KMI = 42° + 42° = 84° \neq 90°$, contradicting $\overleftrightarrow{MI} \perp \overleftrightarrow{KI}$.

Exercise 8

1. Correct. The angles around each point are 97°, 83°, 97°, and 83°, which add to 360°.

2. Incorrect. x could also equal −6.

3. Correct. By a combination of Alternate Interior Angles, Alternate Exterior Angles, and/or Corresponding Angles, the angles around every point A through E are 108°, 72°, 108°, and 72°, which add to 360°.

4. Incorrect. By Alternate Interior Angles followed by Corresponding Angles (or vice versa) the two labeled angles should have the same measure.

Exercise 9

1. Incorrect. The mercury should start at 0° and work its way up.

2. Incorrect. Each interior angle at the base of the triangle equals its vertical angle. So the interior angles are equal (the triangle is isosceles) because the vertical angles are equal (given). So each base angle measures
$$\frac{180° - 72°}{2} = 54°$$
But then the angles around either of the two lower points would be 128°, 54°, 128°, and 54°, which would add to 364° (or 182° for any two consecutive angles).

3. Correct. The sum of the exterior angles is $81° + 137° + 142° = 360°$.

4. Correct. The sum of the exterior angles is $90° + 118° + 152° = 360°$.

Exercise 10

1. Correct. The exterior angles are 90°, 130°, and $180° − 40° = 140°$ (by Vertical Angles), so their sum is $90° + 130° + 140° = 360°$.

2. Correct. The slopes indicate that $\overleftrightarrow{AB} \parallel \overleftrightarrow{DC}$ and $\overleftrightarrow{AC} \perp \overleftrightarrow{BD}$. Because of the parallels, by Alternate Interior Angles $m\angle ABD = 28°$ and $m\angle ACD = 62°$. Because of the perpendiculars, all four angles at the center measure 90°. Then within each triangle, the sums are $90° + 28° + 62° = 180°$.

3. Correct. By Alternate Interior Angles, the lower angle at the lower left vertex is 28°, so the sum of the interior angles of the right triangle is $90° + 62° + 28° = 180°$.

4. Incorrect. The dimensions are too big for the box.

Exercise 11

1. Correct. The two apparently parallel lines are indeed parallel.
$$\text{Slope of } \overleftrightarrow{AE} = \frac{-3 - 6}{-4 - 2} = \frac{3}{2}$$
$$\text{Slope of } \overleftrightarrow{BD} = \frac{-2 - 4}{1 - 5} = \frac{3}{2}$$
So $m\angle AEC = m\angle BDC$, by Corresponding Angles. $m\angle EAC$ and $m\angle DBA$ are supplementary angles. For the two angles to be equal, $\overleftrightarrow{AE}$ and $\overleftrightarrow{BD}$ must be perpendicular to $\overleftrightarrow{AC}$.
$$\text{Slope of } \overleftrightarrow{AC} = \frac{0 - 6}{11 - 2} = \frac{-2}{3}$$
So they are perpendicular and $m\angle EAC = m\angle DBC = 90°$.

2. Incorrect. Perspective is violated at three places—where the upper right front horizontal crosses the back vertical, where the left vertical of the door crosses the lower left rear horizontal, and at the upper left corner of the door. Perspective is possibly also violated at the upper right corner of the door, and possibly also where the upper rear corner meets the roof diagonal.

3. Incorrect. The "equal" angle in the right triangle measures $90° − 37° = 53°$, but the two in the isosceles triangle measure
$$\frac{180° - 54°}{2} = 63°$$

4. Incorrect. The angle adjacent to the 36°
angle must measure 90° − 36° = 54°, either
by Complementary Angles and because a
perpendicular to one of two parallel lines is
perpendicular to the other, or because it is
an alternate interior angle to the third angle
of the smaller right triangle. But it must also
measure 90° − 41° = 49° as the third angle
of the larger right triangle.

Exercise 12

1. Incorrect. The "equal" angle in the left
triangle must measure 180° − 62° − 76° =
42°. But the one in the right triangle must
measure 90° − 38° = 52°.

2. Correct. The angle at the lower left measures
180° − 28° − 52° = 100°.

3. Correct. The missing angle in the left-hand
triangle is 180° − 71° − 58° = 51°, the
missing angle in the right-hand triangle
(which is a right triangle) is 90° − 39° =
51°, and they are equal, as alternate interior
angles should be.

4. Incorrect. This is an impossible object. Cover
any corner with your hand and the other
two corners suggest a skewed (twisted)
object which does not reconnect with itself.

Exercise 13

1. Incorrect. In an isosceles right triangle, the
two equal angles must measure 45°.

2. Incorrect. It takes slightly *more* than 30 years.

$$11.5 \text{ days} \cdot \frac{10^9 \text{ sec}}{10^6 \text{ sec}} \cdot \frac{1 \text{ yr}}{365.25 \text{ days}} \approx 31.49 \text{ yr}$$

3. Incorrect. By the Isosceles Triangle property,
the lower left interior angle of the upper
triangle must also be 36°. Then by Alternate
Interior Angles both missing angles of the
lower triangle must also be 36°. But then the
sum of the interior angles of the lower
triangle would only be 104° + 36° + 36° =
176° ≠ 180°.

4. Correct. The angle adjacent to the 148° angle
must be 32°, whether by the Linear Angles
property (180° − 148° = 32°) or by the
Isosceles Triangle property $\left(\frac{180° − 116°}{2} = 32°\right)$.

Exercise 14

1. Incorrect. By the Isosceles Right Triangle
property, the two missing angles on the
upper triangle measure 45°. Then by
Alternate Interior Angles the missing angle
in the lower triangle also measures 45°. But
by the Interior Angles of a Triangle property
it must measure 180° − 84° − 48° = 48°.

2. Incorrect. By the Isosceles Triangle property,
the angle adjacent to the 18° angle must
measure 52°. Then by Alternate Interior
Angles the missing angle of the left triangle
must also measure 52°. But by Interior
Angles of a Triangle it must measure
180° − 100° − 18° = 62°.

3. Correct. By the Isosceles Triangle property,
the angles adjacent to the upper, horizontal
side must measure 42° and 36° (left to right).
Then by Sum of Interior Angles of a Triangle,
the three angles at the center point must
measure 78°, 102°, and 78° (left to right). This
is consistent with their measures as found by
Vertical Angles and Supplementary Angles.

4. Incorrect. Either the basket is missing one
handle or the one handle is incorrectly
located—it would spill if you held it by the
existing handle.

Exercise 15

1. Incorrect. By the Isosceles Triangle property,
the lower angle of the upper triangle must
measure 52°, so its upper left angle must
measure 180° − 52° − 52° = 76°. Therefore
the "equal" angle in the lower triangle must
also measure 76°. But by the Isosceles
Triangle property, it must measure
$$\frac{180° − 32°}{2} = 74°$$

2. Correct. By the Isosceles Triangle property,
the lower angle of the left-hand triangle
must also measure 76°, so its upper left angle
must measure 180° − 76° − 76° = 28°.
Then the "equal" angle of the right-hand
triangle must also measure 28°, which is
consistent with what it must measure by the
Isosceles Triangle property,
$$\frac{180° − 124°}{2} = 28°$$

© 2003 Key Curriculum Press

What's Wrong with This Picture? Solutions • **53**

3. Incorrect. "Would," "passed," and "Plane" are misspelled.

4. Incorrect. By the Isosceles Triangle property, the upper angle at the top right measures 27°, but this is also an alternate interior angle with respect to the angle labeled 29°.

Exercise 16

1. Correct. The missing angles of the upper left triangle each measure
$$\frac{180° - 150°}{2} = 15°$$
those of the lower right triangle each measure
$$\frac{180° - 62°}{2} = 59°$$
and those of the center triangle measure 59° (by Alternate Interior Angles) and 31° (by Interior Angles of a Triangle). These measures are consistent with $31° + 59° = 90°$, which is true because the base of the upper left triangle is perpendicular to the right-hand line (it is perpendicular to the left-hand line and those two lines are parallel).

2. Incorrect. $124° + 66° + 90° + 90° = 370° \neq 360°$.

3. Incorrect. The dimensions of the laptop are too big.

4. Correct. The angle lowest on the right measures 34° by the Isosceles Triangle property. This is consistent with $56° - 22° = 34°$, where 56° is the missing angle measure of the right-hand right triangle ($90° - 34° = 56°$). The small upper triangles are congruent by AAS, so the lower left angle of the upper left triangle also measures 22°. The remaining angle in each of those triangles measures $90° - 22° = 68°$, consistent with their being vertical angles and with $180° - 112° = 68°$ along either of the diagonals.

Exercise 17

1. Incorrect. "Here's" and "two" are misspelled.

2. Correct. $104° + 76° = 180°$, the sum of two adjacent interior angles in a parallelogram.

3. Incorrect. $104° + 80° + 72° + 114° = 370° \neq 360°$, which should be the sum of the exterior angles of a polygon.

4. Incorrect. The exterior angles corresponding to the three equal angles are all 74°, and the two remaining exterior angles are $180° - 90° = 90°$ and $180° - 138° = 42°$. But $3 \cdot 74° + 90° + 42° = 354° \neq 360°$.

Exercise 18

1. Incorrect. The three marked-equal angles measure $180° - 124° = 56°$, and the other two exterior angles each measure $180° - 90° = 90°$. But $3 \cdot 56° + 2 \cdot 90° = 348° \neq 360°$.

2. Correct. The three angles with a single tick measure $180° - 130° = 50°$, the two with a double tick measure $180° - 120° = 60°$, and the remaining exterior angle is $180° - 90° = 90°$. So $3 \cdot 50° + 2 \cdot 60° + 90° = 360°$.

3. Incorrect. The Jack is a heart on the top left corner and a diamond on the bottom right corner.

4. Correct. In the upper left isosceles triangle, the missing angles each measure
$$\frac{180° - 124°}{2} = 28°$$
In the lower isosceles triangle the missing angles each measure
$$\frac{180° - 72°}{2} = 54°$$
In the quadrilateral, which is a kite, by Symmetry the upper left angle measures 82°. Within the kite, the lower left angle measures $360° - 90° - 2 \cdot 82° = 106°$, which is consistent with $360° - 172° - 28° - 54° = 106°$ around the point of intersection.

Exercise 19

1. Incorrect. The missing interior angle at the bottom center measures $360° - 140° = 220°$. If you were to draw a line connecting the bottom two corners of the quadrilateral, you would have two isosceles triangles, the smaller one with 20° base angles and the larger on with 56° base angles, but $20° + 38° = 58° \neq 56°$.

2. Correct. The inner quadrilateral is a kite, so the non-vertex angles are congruent. So the angle measure at the upper right corner of the outer qudrilateral sum to $28° + 24° + 38° = 90°$. Therefore the angle measure at

the lower left corner of the outer quadrilateral must be 90° by the polygon sum theory. Therefore the outer quadrilateral is a square.

3. Incorrect. In a regular hexagon each interior angle measures $\frac{6-2}{6} \cdot 180° = 120°$. In a regular pentagon each interior angle measures $\frac{5-2}{5} \cdot 180° = 108°$. But at any vertex common to the hexagon and two pentagons shown, the angles sum to $120° + 2 \cdot 108° = 336° \neq 360°$.

4. Incorrect. The curved part of the scissors, where your finger rests, is curved the wrong way and the scissors open the wrong way.

Exercise 20

1. Incorrect. The interior angle corresponding to the 122° angle measures $180° - 122° = 58°$. By Alternate Interior Angles, so does the exterior angle at the top left, and therefore so does the one at the top right. But $122° + 28° + 90° + 2 \cdot 58° = 356° \neq 360°$.

2. Incorrect.
$$\text{Slope of } \overleftrightarrow{BC} = \frac{8-6}{8-0} = \frac{1}{4}$$
$$\text{Slope of } \overleftrightarrow{AD} = \frac{3-0}{12-0} = \frac{1}{4}$$
so the lines are parallel. So by Consecutve Interior Angles the interior angle at C measures $180° - 65° = 115°$. The interior angle at A measures $90° - 14° = 76°$. But $100° + 115° + 65° + 76° = 356° \neq 360°$.

3. Correct. Take the trapezoid at the lower left and extend its upper side to the right until it meets the x-axis under the center of the arch (at the center of the circle). Then the angle at that center is $180° - 2 \cdot 80° = 20°$, so each trapezoid is rotated 20° more than the previous one. Since there are nine trapezoids, the total rotation is $9 \cdot 20° = 180°$, which is correct.

4. Incorrect. The tiger has a lion's mane.

Exercise 21

1. Incorrect. By that logic, there could be a 150% chance of rain in three days, a 200% chance of rain in four days, and so on, and "a 150% chance" or "a 200% chance" doesn't make any sense.

2. Incorrect. The 24° inscribed angle subtends a $2 \cdot 24° = 48°$ arc. But $126° + 48° + 180° = 354° \neq 360°$.

3. Incorrect. The congruent chords subtend congruent arcs, so the arc on the left also measures 130°. The 40° inscribed angle subtends an arc measuring $2 \cdot 40° = 80°$. But $80° + 2 \cdot 130° = 340° \neq 360°$.

4. Correct. The 75° inscribed angle subtends an arc of $2 \cdot 75° = 150°$, and $150° + 90° + 120° = 360°$.

Exercise 22

1. Correct. $\triangle NTO$ is a right triangle with right angle at point T, since $\overrightarrow{NT}$ is a tangent. In the triangle, $m\angle NOT = 90° - 36° = 54°$, consistent with $360° - 306° = 54°$ around O.

2. Incorrect. $\angle ARO$ and $\angle AYO$ are both right angles since $\overrightarrow{AR}$ and $\overrightarrow{AY}$ are tangents. But $148° + 42° + 90° + 90° = 370° \neq 360°$.

3. Correct. It *is* false.
$$|x+3| = \begin{cases} x+3, & x+3 \geq 0 \\ -(x+3), & x+3 < 0 \end{cases}$$
$$= \begin{cases} x+3, & x \geq -3 \\ -x-3, & x < -3 \end{cases}$$

4. Incorrect. Parallel chords subtend equal arcs, so the arc on the left also measures 76°. But $88° + 124° + 2 \cdot 76° = 364° \neq 360°$.

Exercise 23

1. Incorrect. Chords of equal length subtend arcs of equal lengths, so the arc on the right also measures 71°. But $71° + 71° + 2 \cdot 37° + 2 \cdot 76° = 368° \neq 360°$.

2. Incorrect. Since the quadrilateral is a parallelogram, the angle opposite the 85° angle must also measure 85°, so each inscribed angle must subtend an arc measuring $2 \cdot 85° = 170°$. But $2 \cdot 170° = 340° \neq 360°$. (Also, the only parallelogram that you can inscribe in a circle is a rectangle. This is because the distances from the center of the parallelogram—the intersection of the diagonals—to the vertices must be radii, and therefore equal in length; only in a rectangle are they equal.)

3. Incorrect. The claw of the hammer is reversed.

4. Correct. The larger arc measures $360° - 141° = 219°$, so the exterior angle should measure $\frac{1}{2}(219° - 141°) = 39°$, which it does.

Exercise 24

1. Incorrect. By the Inscribed Angle theorem, $2 \cdot 77° + 2 \cdot 113° = 380° \neq 360°$.

2. Incorrect. "Chile" is really Peru, "Peru" is really Brazil, "Brazil" is really Bolivia, and "Bolivia" is really Chile.

3. Incorrect. $m\overarc{SQ} = m\overarc{TR} = 90°$ since both are subtended by 90° central angles.

4. Correct. A central right angle subtends a quarter of the circle, and
$$\frac{1}{4} \cdot 2\pi r = \frac{\pi r}{2} = \frac{\pi \cdot 10 \text{ cm}}{2} = 5\pi \text{ cm}$$

Exercise 25

1. Incorrect. The lines should be parallel since the alternate interior angles are equal. But
$$\text{Slope of } \overleftrightarrow{SE} = \frac{4 - 2}{-1 - (-4)} = \frac{2}{3}$$
$$\text{and Slope of } \overleftrightarrow{TC} = \frac{1 - (-3)}{5 - (-2)} = \frac{4}{7} \neq \frac{2}{3}$$

2. Correct. Each rhombus is made of two congruent equilateral triangles, and hence has two interior angles measuring 60° each and two measuring 120° each. At the junction of three rhombuses we have $3 \cdot 120° = 360°$, and at the junction of six rhombuses $6 \cdot 60° = 360°$.

3. Correct. First, $BR = QR - BQ = 16 - 6 = 10$. Next, $DP = AP$, $AQ = BQ$, $CR = BR$, and $CS = DS$, since they are pairs of tangents from the same point. Then $2(10 + 6 + 10 + 8) = 68$.

4. Incorrect. "Dictionary" is spelled wrong, and the perspective of the back leg of the table is wrong.

Exercise 26

1. Incorrect. The wheelbarrow has only one handle.

2. Incorrect. The left side measures $12 \text{ cm} + 6 \text{ cm} = 18 \text{ cm}$, and the bottom measures $10 \text{ cm} + 18 \text{ cm} = 28 \text{ cm}$. The perimeter is $2(10 \text{ cm} + 18 \text{ cm} + 12 \text{ cm} + 6 \text{ cm}) = 92 \text{ cm}$, which is correct, but $(28 \text{ cm})(18 \text{ cm}) - (6 \text{ cm})(18 \text{ cm}) = 396 \text{ cm}^2 \neq 504 \text{ cm}^2$.

3. Incorrect. The triangles are all 3-4-5 triangles ($36 + 64 = 100$, and $36\text{-}48\text{-}60 = 48\text{-}64\text{-}80 = 60\text{-}80\text{-}100 = 3\text{-}4\text{-}5$), and therefore right triangles. But $A = \frac{1}{2} \cdot (60 \text{ cm})(80 \text{ cm}) = 2400 \text{ cm}^2 \neq 4800 \text{ cm}^2$.

4. Correct. $C = 2\pi r = 2\pi(12 \text{ cm}) = 24\pi \text{ cm}$ and $A = \pi r^2 = \pi(12 \text{ cm})^2 = 144\pi \text{ cm}^2$.

Exercise 27

1. Incorrect. $2(6 \text{ cm})(7 \text{ cm}) + (12 \text{ cm})(6 \text{ cm}) = 156 \text{ cm}^2 \neq 114 \text{ cm}^2$.

2. Incorrect. The top of the drawing shows three round pillars, and the bottom shows two square ones.

3. Correct. $A = 2 \cdot \pi r^2 + 2\pi r \cdot h = 2\pi(6 \text{ cm})^2 + 2\pi(6 \text{ cm})(12 \text{ cm}) = 216\pi \text{ cm}^2$.

4. Incorrect. $2 \cdot \frac{1}{2}(6 \text{ cm})(8 \text{ cm}) + (8 \text{ cm})(18 \text{ cm}) + (6 \text{ cm})(18 \text{ cm}) + (10 \text{ cm})(18 \text{ cm}) = 480 \text{ cm}^2 \neq 300 \text{ cm}^2$.

Exercise 28

1. Incorrect. The missing side is $40 \text{ cm} - 2 \cdot (8 \text{ cm}) = 24 \text{ cm}$. $P = 40 \text{ cm} + 24 \text{ cm} + 2 \cdot (17 \text{ cm}) = 98 \text{ cm}$, which is correct, but
$$A = h \cdot \frac{b_1 + b_2}{2}$$
$$= (15 \text{ cm}) \cdot \frac{40 \text{ cm} + 24 \text{ cm}}{2}$$
$$= 480 \text{ cm}^2 \neq 544 \text{ cm}^2$$

2. Incorrect. A central right angle subtends a quarter of a circle.
$$P = 2 \cdot r + \frac{1}{4} \cdot 2\pi r$$
$$= 2r + \frac{\pi r}{2}$$
$$= 2 \cdot (8 \text{ cm}) + \frac{\pi \cdot (8 \text{ cm})}{2}$$
$$= (16 + 4\pi) \text{ cm}$$
which is correct. But
$$A = \frac{1}{4} \cdot \pi r^2$$
$$= \frac{1}{4} \cdot \pi \cdot (8 \text{ cm})^2$$
$$= 16\pi \text{ cm}^2$$
$$\neq 64\pi \text{ cm}^2$$

3. Correct. Each interior angle of a square measures 90°, and each interior angle of an octagon measures $\frac{8-2}{8} \cdot 180° = 135°$. At each vertex, $90° + 2 \cdot 135° = 360°$.

4. Incorrect. If the figure is a rectangle, the base measures

$$\frac{96 \text{ cm}^2}{12 \text{ cm}} = 8 \text{ cm}$$

so the perimeter is $P = 2(12 \text{ cm} + 8 \text{ cm}) = 40 \text{ cm}$, which is correct. But the shaded area $A = \frac{1}{2} \cdot \pi (4 \text{ cm})^2 + \frac{1}{2} \cdot \pi (6 \text{ cm})^2 = 26\pi \text{ cm}^2 \neq 52\pi \text{ cm}^2$.

Exercise 29

1. Correct. If the chunk were not missing, we would have $a = 2[(10 \text{ cm})(20 \text{ cm}) + (10 \text{ cm})(15 \text{ cm}) + (15 \text{ cm})(20 \text{ cm})] = 1300 \text{ cm}^2$. The surfaces created by taking out the chunk are equal in surface area and maintain the same surface area for the object.

2. Incorrect.

$$\frac{1}{2} \cdot GA = \frac{3\sqrt{3} \text{ cm}}{\sqrt{3}} = 3 \text{ cm}$$

so $GA = 6 \text{ cm}$, and perimeter $P = 6 \cdot (6 \text{ cm}) = 36 \text{ cm} \neq 72 \text{ cm}$. Also,

$$\text{Area} = 6 \cdot \frac{1}{2} \cdot bh = 3(6 \text{ cm})(3\sqrt{3} \text{ cm})$$
$$= 54\sqrt{3} \text{ cm}^2 \neq 384\sqrt{3} \text{ cm}^2$$

3. Incorrect. Book pages are typically numbered with even numbers on the left and odd numbers on the right.

4. Incorrect. The upper triangular half of the quadrilateral is an isosceles triangle, so its base angles are

$$\frac{180° - 60°}{2} = 60°$$

So it is actually an equiangular/equilateral triangle. Therefore, its base, which is the horizontal diagonal of the quadrilateral, is also 12 cm. But 3 cm + 8 cm = 11 cm < 12 cm, so the figure is impossible.

Exercise 30

1. Incorrect. For a 30°-60°-90° triangle the proportions should be 1-$\sqrt{3}$-2, so either 12-12$\sqrt{3}$-24 or 10-10$\sqrt{3}$-20.

2. Incorrect. France and Spain are switched, switching Paris and Madrid along with them.

3. Incorrect. For a 30°-60°-90° triangle the proportions should be 1-$\sqrt{3}$-2, so we should have 18-18$\sqrt{3}$-36 rather than 18-18$\sqrt{2}$-36.

4. Correct. For an isosceles right triangle, the proportions are 1-1-$\sqrt{2}$, and 72-72-72$\sqrt{2}$ = 1-1-$\sqrt{2}$.

Exercise 31

1. Correct. It *is* false, since $x^2 \leq x$ for $0 \leq x \leq 1$.

2. Incorrect. $8^2 + 15^2 = 289 = 17^2 \neq 18^2$.

3. Correct. $14^2 + 48^2 = 2500 = 50^2$. This is a 7-24-25 triangle.

4. Incorrect. In an isosceles right triangle, each of the other two angles should be 45°, not 40°.

Exercise 32

1. Incorrect. Each side of the quadrilateral has length $s = \sqrt{576 \text{ cm}^2} = 24 \text{ cm}$, and the diagonal, $d = \sqrt{(24 \text{ cm})^2 + (24 \text{ cm})^2}$, which is correct. But $P = 4 \cdot (24 \text{ cm}) = 96 \text{ cm} \neq 48 \text{ cm}$.

2. Incorrect. The upper triangle is proportional to a 3-4-5 right triangle, so the missing side is 10. But that means the lower triangle is an isosceles right triangle, which should be 1-1-$\sqrt{2}$, so its hypotenuse should be 10$\sqrt{2}$, not 10$\sqrt{3}$.

3. Incorrect. The seven and eight of spades each include a heart symbol.

4. Correct. The upper triangle is a right triangle, so its missing side is $\sqrt{(80)^2 + (150)^2} = 170$ (it's an 8-15-17 triangle). The lower triangle is a 30°-60°-90° triangle, so its proportions should be 1-$\sqrt{3}$-2, and 85-85$\sqrt{3}$-170 = 1-$\sqrt{3}$-2.

Exercise 33

1. Incorrect. In an equilateral triangle, $h = \frac{1}{2} \cdot b \cdot \sqrt{3}$, so the height should be 9$\sqrt{3}$ cm, not 9$\sqrt{2}$ cm.

2. Incorrect. The handle of the pencil sharpener is going the wrong way, and the perspective of the back leg of the table is wrong.

3. Correct. Divide each small triangle in half by bisecting each 36 cm base. Then the new small triangles are 30°-60°-90° triangles,

© 2003 Key Curriculum Press

What's Wrong with This Picture? Solutions • 57

with the proportions $1\text{-}\sqrt{3}\text{-}2$, so they must be $6\sqrt{3}\text{-}18\text{-}12\sqrt{3} = 1\text{-}\sqrt{3}\text{-}2$. Thus the radius is $12\sqrt{3}$ cm, so area of circle $= \pi r^2 = \pi(12\sqrt{3} \text{ cm})^2 = 432\pi \text{ cm}^2$. The altitude of the inscribed triangle is $6\sqrt{3}$ cm $+ 12\sqrt{3}$ cm $= 18\sqrt{3}$ cm, so area of equilateral triangle $= \frac{1}{2}bh = \frac{1}{2} \cdot (36 \text{ cm})(18\sqrt{3} \text{ cm}) = 324\sqrt{3} \text{ cm}^2$.

4. Correct. In the 30°-60°-90° right triangle, the base is 32 cm $-$ 20 cm $=$ 12 cm, and the sides must be in the proportion $1\text{-}\sqrt{3}\text{-}2$, so they must be $12\text{-}12\sqrt{3}\text{-}24 = 1\text{-}\sqrt{3}\text{-}2$. Then the hypotenuse of the largest right triangle must be $\sqrt{(32 \text{ cm})^2 + (12\sqrt{3} \text{ cm})^2} = \sqrt{1456 \text{ cm}^2} = 4\sqrt{91}$ cm. Then $A = \frac{1}{2}bh = \frac{1}{2}(20 \text{ cm})(12\sqrt{3} \text{ cm}) = 120\sqrt{3} \text{ cm}^2$, and $P = 20$ cm $+$ 24 cm $+ 4\sqrt{91}$ cm $= (44 + 4\sqrt{91})$ cm.

Exercise 34

1. Correct. $\sqrt{3^2 + 4^2 + 12^2} = \sqrt{169} = 13$.

2. Incorrect. This is another impossible figure. From the left, it looks as though there are four prongs to the tuning fork, but from the right, there are three.

3. Correct. The small right triangle is an 8-15-17 triangle $(8^2 + 15^2 = 17^2)$. The base of the large right triangle is $8 + 12 = 20$, so the large triangle is a 15-20-25 $=$ 3-4-5 triangle $(15^2 + 20^2 = 25^2)$.

4. Incorrect. The base of each right triangle is
$$\frac{118 \text{ cm} - 90 \text{ cm}}{2} = 14 \text{ cm}$$
so each right triangle is a 14-48-50 $=$ 7-24-25 triangle $(50^2 - 14^2 = 48^2)$. The height is 48 cm, so
$$A = h \cdot \frac{b_1 + b_2}{2}$$
$$= (48 \text{ cm}) \cdot \frac{118 \text{ cm} + 90 \text{ cm}}{2}$$
$$= 4992 \text{ cm}^2 \neq 392 \text{ cm}^2$$

Exercise 35

1. Incorrect. "Where" and "bored" are misspelled.

2. Incorrect. The triangular base is an 8-15-17 triangle $(8^2 + 15^2 = 17^2)$, so $V = BH =$

$(\frac{1}{2}bh)H = \frac{1}{2}(8 \text{ cm})(15 \text{ cm})(10 \text{ cm}) = 600 \text{ cm}^3 \neq 680 \text{ cm}^3$.

3. Correct. $l = \frac{V}{wh} = \frac{480 \text{ cm}^3}{(12 \text{ cm})(4 \text{ cm})} = 10$ cm, so Surface area $= 2[(4 \text{ cm})(10 \text{ cm}) + (4 \text{ cm})(12 \text{ cm}) + (10 \text{ cm})(12 \text{ cm})] = 416 \text{ cm}^2$.

4. Incorrect. $V = lwh = (12 \text{ cm})(4 \text{ cm})(6 \text{ cm}) = 288 \text{ cm}^3$, not cm^2, as shown.

Exercise 36

1. Incorrect. $V = \frac{1}{3}Bh = \frac{1}{3}(210 \text{ cm}^2)(12 \text{ cm}) = 840 \text{ cm}^3 \neq 1260 \text{ cm}^3$.

2. Incorrect. $V = BH = (\frac{1}{2}bh)H = \frac{1}{2}(6 \text{ cm})(8 \text{ cm})(4 \text{ cm}) = 96 \text{ cm}^3$, which is correct, but the diagonal is 10 cm (6-8-10 $=$ 3-4-5), so Surface area $= (4 \text{ cm})(6 \text{ cm}) + (4 \text{ cm})(8 \text{ cm}) + (4 \text{ cm})(10 \text{ cm}) + 2 \cdot \frac{1}{2}(6 \text{ cm})(8 \text{ cm}) = 144 \text{ cm}^2 \neq 96 \text{ cm}^2$.

3. Correct. It *is* true, because
$$(\sqrt{3} - \sqrt{2})(\sqrt{3} + \sqrt{2}) = (\sqrt{3})^2 - (\sqrt{2})^2$$
$$= 3 - 2 = 1$$

4. Incorrect. The triangle is a 12-16-20 $=$ 3-4-5 triangle, so the radius is $\frac{20 \text{ cm}}{2} = 10$ cm, so $A = \frac{1}{2} \times \pi r^2 = \frac{1}{2}\pi(10 \text{ cm})^2 = 50\pi \text{ cm}^2 \neq 100 \text{ cm}^2$.

Exercise 37

1. Incorrect. The triangle *is* a right triangle, since 6-8-10 $=$ 3-4-5. Also,
$$V = \frac{1}{3}Bh$$
$$= \frac{1}{3}(\pi r^2)h$$
$$= \frac{1}{3}\pi(6 \text{ cm})^2(8 \text{ cm})$$
$$= 96\pi \text{ cm}^3$$
which is correct. However, in a 30°-60°-90° triangle, the proportions should be $1\text{-}\sqrt{3}\text{-}2$, not 6-8-10 $=$ 3-4-5. For the proportions shown, the actual angle is $\approx 53.1301°$.

2. Correct. $B = \pi r^2 = 36\pi \Rightarrow r = 6$ cm, so the triangle is 6-8-10 $=$ 3-4-5. With $h = 8$ cm, $V = \frac{1}{3}Bh = \frac{1}{3}(36\pi \text{ cm}^2)(8 \text{ cm}) = 96\pi \text{ cm}^3$.

3. Incorrect. The "3" is backward and the hour hand ought to be about one-third of the way from the "8" toward the "9."

4. Correct. The missing chunk is $(12 - 7)$ cm by $(8 - 4)$ cm by 2 cm, or 5 cm by 4 cm by 2 cm, so $V = (12\text{ cm})(8\text{ cm})(2\text{ cm}) - (5\text{ cm})(4\text{ cm})(2\text{ cm}) = 152\text{ cm}^3$.

Exercise 38

1. Incorrect. The tips of the rake are pointing both ways.

2. Correct.
$$B = h \cdot \frac{b_1 + b_2}{2}$$
$$= (4\text{ cm}) \cdot \frac{14\text{ cm} + 7\text{ cm}}{2}$$
$$= 42\text{ cm}^2$$
and $V = BH = (42\text{ cm}^2)(10\text{ cm}) = 420\text{ cm}^3$.

3. Incorrect. The right triangle is a 7-24-25 triangle ($25^2 - 7^2 = 24^2$), so the height is 24 cm. $V = BH = (\pi r^2)H = \pi(4\text{ cm})^2(24\text{ cm}) = 384\pi\text{ cm}^3 \neq 400\pi\text{ cm}^3$

4. Incorrect. To calculate the volume, one must subtract the volume of the "bite" from that of the simple rectangle solid. The height is 6 cm + 4 cm = 10 cm, so $V = (12\text{ cm})(2\text{ cm})(10\text{ cm}) - (3\text{ cm})(2\text{ cm})(4\text{ cm}) = 216\text{ cm}^3 \neq 240\text{ cm}^3$.

Exercise 39

1. Incorrect. By Alternate Interior Angles, the unmarked angle at C (above $\overleftrightarrow{CD}$) measures 68° and $m\angle BCD = 58°$. $\therefore m\angle BCA = 58°$. But then in $\triangle ABC$, $68° + 2 \cdot 58° = 184° \neq 180°$.

2. Correct. Because the figure is a kite, the vertical diagonal must bisect the horizontal diagonal, so the left half of the horizontal diagonal must also measure 15 cm. The measurements are consistent with right triangles: 15-20-25 = 3-4-5 and 15-36-39 = 5-12-13.

3. Incorrect. The dog has a rat tail.

4. Correct. This is a correct analysis.

Exercise 40

1. Incorrect. These are similar triangles, by AAA, but 8:9 ≠ 6:7.

2. Correct. This is a correct analysis.

3. Correct. $V = BH = (\pi R^2 - \pi r^2)H = \pi H(R^2 - r^2) = \pi(4\text{ cm})[(6\text{ cm})^2 - (3\text{ cm}^2)] = 108\pi\text{ cm}^3$.

4. Incorrect. The tree's shadow points one way, and the shadows of the man and the mailbox point a different way.

Exercise 41

1. Incorrect. The saddle is on backward.

2. Incorrect. The triangles are supposed to be similar, because 7-9-10 = 14-18-20. But then the two corresponding angles shown should be equal.

3. Incorrect. The analysis is correct, but the arithmetic is incorrect. The last two lines of calculation should show $6x = 96$ and $x = 16$.

4. Correct. $V = \frac{1}{3}BH = \frac{1}{3}(120\text{ cm}^2)(18\text{ cm}) = 720\text{ cm}^3$.

Exercise 42

1. Incorrect. Note the direction of the inequality sign. The last two lines of calculation should be $3x \leq 6$; $x \leq 2$.

2. Incorrect. The solution should be $\frac{8}{12 + 8} = \frac{x}{15}$; $x = 6$.

3. Correct. Both the analysis and the arithmetic are correct.

4. Incorrect. The solution should be $\left(\frac{3}{5}\right)^2 = \frac{18}{A}$; $9A = 450$; $A = 50$.

Exercise 43

1. Correct. Both the analysis and the arithmetic are correct.

2. Incorrect. The sides of the triangle are correct for a right triangle (35-84-91 = 5-12-13), but $\tan^{-1}\frac{84}{35} \approx 67.3801° \neq 57°$.

3. Incorrect. The batter is on the wrong side of the plate, given the direction of his swing.

4. Incorrect. A 3-4-5 triangle is not the same as a 30°-60°-90° triangle, where one leg is half the other. Also, $\tan^{-1}\frac{4}{3} \approx 53.1301° \neq 60°$.

Exercise 44

1. Correct. An 8-15-17 triangle *is* a right triangle ($17^2 - 8^2 = 15^2$), and the trigonometric ratios are defined correctly.

2. Incorrect. The two triangles have a pair of corresponding angles, but the given side

© 2003 Key Curriculum Press

What's Wrong with This Picture? Solutions • 59

lengths are not proportional. So the properties of similar triangles do not apply.

3. Incorrect. The solution should be $\tan 26° = \frac{x}{48}$; $x = 48(\tan 26°)$; $x \approx 23$.

4. Incorrect. The chicken has webbed feet (like a duck).

Exercise 45

1. Correct. The number of rectangles is a "triangular" number, and the nth triangular number $t_n = \frac{n(n+1)}{2}$, so $A = \frac{n(n+1)}{2}ab = \frac{10(10+1)}{2}ab = 55ab$.

2. Correct. A 60° wedge removes $\frac{1}{6}$ of the volume, so $V = \frac{5}{6}\pi r^2 h = \frac{5}{6}\pi(6\text{ cm})^2(6\text{ cm}) = 180\pi \text{ cm}^3$.

3. Incorrect. This would be true if $\overline{CD}$ were the bisector of the *base*, not the *angle* or if the triangle was isoceles.

4. Correct. Both the analysis and the arithmetic are correct.

Exercise 46

1. Correct. Both the analysis and the algebra are correct.

2. Incorrect. The very first line of the solution is wrong. (3, 4) is the *midpoint* of $\overline{AD}$, and the altitude doesn't necessarily go to the midpoint. The next three lines are correct. But you need to substitute $A(-2, 0)$, not $D(3, 4)$, into the equation. So $0 = \frac{3}{4}(-2) + b \Rightarrow b = \frac{3}{2} \Rightarrow y = \frac{3}{4}x + \frac{3}{2}$, or $3x - 4y = -6$.

3. Incorrect. The line segment a bisects the angle, so "72°" should be $\frac{72°}{2} = 36°$ everywhere in the solution. This gives Area $= \frac{1}{2} \cdot \frac{12}{\tan 36°}(24 \cdot 5) \approx 991 \text{ cm}^2$.

Exercise 47

1. Correct. The given transformation does produce the given result.

2. Correct. The transformation is applied correctly.

3. Incorrect. $P = 2(24 \text{ cm} + 13 \text{ cm}) = 74 \text{ cm}$, which is correct, but $A = (12 \text{ cm})(24 \text{ cm}) = 288 \text{ cm}^2 \neq 312 \text{ cm}^2$.

4. Correct. The rotation has been done correctly.

Exercise 48

1. Incorrect. In general, you can't multiply units by themselves to give any "meaningful" units (with the exception of units of length). This proof "proved" that 1 "*square* pound" equals 256 "*square* ounces," which is meaningless.

2. Correct. The outline is correct, but could use more detail. Underneath "$\overline{CD}$ is a median (Given)," we need "$\overline{AB}$ is bisected at D (Definition of median)," followed by "$\overline{AD} \cong \overline{BD}$ (Definition of line segment bisector)." Then that connects to "$\triangle ADC \cong \triangle BDC$ (SSS)," and the rest of the proof is correct.

3. Correct. The analysis and the algebra are correct.

Exercise 49

1. Correct.

2. Incorrect. Both knobs are labeled "H."

3. Correct. Both the analysis and the algebra are correct.

Exercise 50

1. Incorrect. The proof mistakenly assumes that $\overline{CD}$ intersects the two circles in two *distinct* points E and F, but in fact it can be shown that $\overline{CD}$ will always intersect *both* circles at B. Thus there is only *one* perpendicular, namely $\overline{AB}$.

2. Correct.

3. Correct. Let A and B be the midpoints of $\overline{FO}$ and $\overline{UR}$ respectively. Then a point is closer to an endpoint than it is to O or U if the point is on $\overline{FA}$ or on $\overline{BR}$. Because $FA = BR = \frac{1}{6}FR$, the probability of a point being on one of those segments is

$$\frac{\frac{1}{6}FR + \frac{1}{6}FR}{FR} = \frac{1}{3}$$

(Note that if the random point coincides with A or B, it would then be equidistant, rather than closer to an endpoint. But omitting those two points subtracts a length of $2 \cdot 0 = 0$, because a point has no length, so the answer is not changed.)